DIGGING INTO SOUTH TEXAS PREHISTORY

DIGGING INTO SOUTH TEXAS PREHISTORY

A GUIDE FOR AMATEUR ARCHAEOLOGISTS

THOMAS R. HESTER

Preface by John Graves

Corona Publishing Company
San Antonio, Texas
1980

Library of Congress Catalog Card No. 79-55641
ISBN 0-931722-05-5

Cover illustration by Michael E. Morrow
Cover design by Paul Hudgins
Book design and layout by Patricia Broersma

Printed and bound in the United States of America

For Wade House and T. C. Hill, Jr.

PREFACE

Most modern American retrospection, my own as a writer included, has been confined to historic times on this particular continent, for during the nearly five centuries that have passed since Caucasians began landing purposefully on these shores enough has happened, uproarious or otherwise, to give any backward-looker plenty of fuel for thought. Yet "our" people didn't encounter a cultural vacuum when they got to North America, a place where human beings were merely an unemphatic part of the landscape. True, reading most history written before the last couple of generations or so might make you think that such had been the case, for it is only rather lately that the customs and procedence of red men, who had pretty much ruled here for a good many thousands of years before we came, have been of much interest to anyone but a few scholarly types housed in the Smithsonian and other musty places.

Astoundingly—so the general belief ran—these indigenous primitives had refused to welcome progress when it showed up in the form of white men and thus had made themselves the Enemy to be fought down and extirpated, as indeed was done. Though the best of them were endowed perhaps with qualities of Noble Savagery and were elegized by Longfellow, Cooper, et al., they were nonetheless rightly doomed by their own pigheaded backwardness, their adherence to outworn habits and views. Besides, they were in the way.

I don't find it possible to wax very indignant about this slanted version of our history that for so long prevailed. We have in fact grown mainly out of Euro-American traditions, and a notable part of any civilization's lore is laced together with cultural self-justification and the bad-mouthing of other breeds, as witness so many of the Old Testament's aggressively Hebraic tales and sagas. The history and legends of the other breeds—the losers—have nearly always tended to be submerged and obscured, even to vanish. Most of what comes down to later ages as truth is the annals of winners, even if the winning is indirect or accidental, as when a body of Jewish legend was taken over by burgeoning Christianity and passed along through the centuries to much of our present world. The story of David is a part of Western consciousness; the exploits of Babylonian Gilgamesh lay deeply buried as inscriptions on clay tablets till dug up and deciphered in modern times—what was left of them. In our own home region of Texas, the spotty records pertaining to early Spanish visitors like Coronado and Cabeza de Vaca have received exhaustive attention and interpretation, and by law are made known to every schoolchild, while the diverse and pristine Indian cultures among which these men wandered have receded into mist.

A recent shift in attitudes, a sharpening of our interest in the Stone Age losers who preceded us in and on this land, may be in some sense a sign of approaching cultural maturity and generosity on our part, a willingness to concede that other people's ways and lore can have had importance for their own sake. Less nobly, though, this interest may also be traceable in large part to a growing and goosey awareness that the progress we and our ancestors have believed ourselves to represent has not led unambiguously toward Utopia, but at least partly in the other direction.

In Texas, for instance—or what we now call Texas—red men lived successfully for nine or ten or no one yet knows how many thousands of years before we burst into view with Manifest Destiny on our minds. They not only survived here but adapted to climatic change and increased in numbers, taking on new tools and ways as time went on, and they did all this without making many bad dents in the natural shape of things. The matrix of life, the blessed and complex regimen of soil and water and grass and trees that gave sustenance to all creatures human and otherwise, varied a bit from natural influences but appears to have remained fully functional from the end of the Ice Age until technologically advanced white men really got moving here with cash-crop agriculture and large-scale cattle raising. Then, in less than 150 years in most parts of the state, much of the land was denuded of its grass and timber and other cover, soil washed and blew away, the water cycle was disastrously altered, and the long-term productivity of the land shrank hugely.

This truly catastrophic change is still in progress and it is tempting to ascribe it, as some current purists do, to a basic and mystic difference between the two breeds of men, to an awareness—lacking in those of European stock but dominant in Amerinds—of the sacred wholeness of nature and the need to maintain it intact. Unfortunately such a theory won't wash. It seems fairly clear that in nearly all parts of the world, the extent of diminution and destruction of natural richness at the hands of men has been dependent on three main factors. One is the vulnerability of individual regions to destruction, since hilly and mountainous and arid lands are far more easily damaged than are flat, well-watered, more or less self-healing places like the American Midwest and much of temperate Europe. Another is the number of men involved. And the third is how much technological sophistication the men in question bring to the joyous task of destruction, because if they've got it they're going to use it.

According to some respectable scholars, even our sparse and ecologically virtuous Paleo-Indians, using atlatl and short spear and cooperative hunting techniques, may have hastened the extinction of such big meat creatures as mammoths and giant bison and ground sloths. Their later cousins the Aztecs were busily decimating the soils on Mexican mountain slopes, by the way they chose to farm maize, a good long while before Hernán Cortez and his tough, grabby, unecological band of cohorts came along with spurs a-jingling. Plains Indians like our Comanches, suddenly made dynamic by the acquisition of horses, would almost certainly have used that new technology destructively against the buffalo and other resources of the wide grasslands, as they did use it against less warlike red neighbors, if white men had only stayed away from the region long enough to let them work out the details of that destiny.

Nevertheless red men *were* here for those thousands of years, and for the most part they were here gently. In practical terms, it matters that this was so. For in a day when we latecomers in this land, through whose abundance we have so briefly and happily and ruinously ripped and romped, are wondering how to patch up the damage a bit and how to learn to live permanently and reasonably well with what is here, it behooves us to get as good a look as we can at people who did achieve this.

****

There is also the perhaps impractical matter of ghosts. Among the many people I've known who cared strongly about a piece of land or a stretch of country, whether or not they owned it, some few have been interested solely in the land as land, in its fauna and soils and flora and its possibilities economic or otherwise, and not at all in human beings' bygone presence on it. But not many. Most of us, even fairly hermitish types, are more sociable than that and spend a certain amount of time wondering about our predecessors in these localities, studying whatever traces they've left, trying to puzzle out who they were and what they were like as people. To know a bit about these things somehow makes the land a wholer place for us.

If you're from the general region in question yourself with its people in your background, you can usually do a fair job of interpreting the signs and relics of white people who were here before you. Through courthouse records and local histories and neighborhood gossip you can often learn their names, and what reputations they had, and which of them ran off to California in 1909 leaving an ailing wife and eight youngsters on the mortgaged place. Their rusty broken spurs and harness buckles and implements, their patent medicine bottles and dish fragments and cartridge cases and Model T parts lie embedded in the surface of the soil; near a jumble of squared foundation stones that represent a house they once lived in, you find a heap of stove ashes, a clump of still thriving lantana, a Levi Garrett three-dot snuff jar, and maybe a half-collapsed storm cellar where rattlesnakes seek dark shade in August. From all such evidence and from childhood memory of people like these you know a good deal about them. You have intimacy with their ghosts.

Red ghosts are less easy to come at. They left no explicit records: no courthouse files, no county histories, no clay tablets incised with the feats of tribal heroes. Being hunters and gatherers in most of Texas, they didn't even stay in one spot for very long at a time, though they must have come back to good spots seasonally year after year. During the thousands of years of their presence, a number of different kinds of them came to these spots, and the earlier kinds were probably as much of a mystery to those who came afterward as the whole array of them is to us. Except that they all had something in common with one another, something we modern usurpers can perceive only dimly and by dint of much pondering and effort. From the earliest of them to the most recent, they had a total dependence on these very local areas of land as the land then was, and a necessary intimate knowledge of its ways and vegetation and creatures and how all these could be put to human use. Their lore was of hills and streams and wild live things and storms and trees and medicinal plants, much of it undoubtedly sacred in tone. They lived by it and because of it, and mainly it vanished when they did.

Sometimes, though, a smell of them seeps through the haze of years, allied most often—for me at any rate—with a whiff, a glimpse, a sense of the land itself as it used to be. On the hilly, battered stock farm in North Central Texas where I now live, part of an area that wore out fast in frontier days because its sloping soils washed away easily when bared by casual farming and overgrazing, obvious Indian traces are scarce. Much relevant material must have washed away with the dirt in the time of destruction, and what remained has often been scattered by bulldozers clearing invasive cedar brush. But a sharp eye can pick out things now and then, and two or three years ago one of my daughters found indications of what could have been a fair-sized camp on a rocky nose overlooking our creek.

At that point the stream runs over scoured bare limestone, with a low dirt cut bank on one side and on the other, where it has undermined the nose itself, great boulders strewn down a naked stone slope that is almost a cliff, with scraggly cedars rooted in cracks of the mother rock. It is one of the prettiest spots on our place, and just below it the creek drops off a ledge in a waterfall high enough to sit under at evening while the flow massages your tired shoulders and washes away the day's grime. Flood-sculptured and weather-grayed, all that stoniness seems eternal, something that must always have looked just as it does now. But it didn't. The clue to what the spot used to be like, not long ago as the land measures time, is the same clue that revealed the Indian site to a teenager's probing eye: thousands of bits of white mussel shell dropped by aborigines on the high nose and showing as far as the edge of the almost-cliff.

Mussels inhabit steady, dependable streams with soft bottoms of sand or mud into which they can burrow, and there is no such bottom anywhere in our mile of the creek today, or a single mussel either. There can't be, because the creek's steadiness ceased with the destruction of the hills' water-rationing mat of grasses and topsoil in the early years of the region's use by whites. These days it is what hydrologists call a "flashy" stream, trickling at best during dry spells and raging after big rains, sluicing away all fine sediments, gnawing its channel and banks with grinding gravel and stones. It is a restless, changing thing; even its waterfall has moved upstream fifteen feet or more in the twenty years since we came here, as rises abrade its ledge.

But, fingering bits of shell and flint and coming across occasional tool or weapon fragments, with a sort of major forced leap of the imagination you can summon up a time when both banks, cloaked in good soil and grass and big creekshore trees, sloped more gently down to a slower sand-bottomed stream that ran pleasantly all year long, dry years and wet, because it was fed steadily by cool seep springs along its banks and those of tributary branches, the rationed downflow of rainwater hoarded in spongy soil throughout the 10,000 acres or so of the creek's drainage basin. In such a place fish and molluscs and crustaceans teemed, as did game animals and birds on the tallgrass uplands; in fact this abundance lasted into historic times and is noted in the writings of whites who passed through the neighborhood in pre-settlement days.

Thus it seems doubtful that they had to work hard for a living, the red men who came to this creek. They had some time to rest and dream and talk and think, time to study and learn, as I myself have dreamed and thought and studied here also but without benefit of tribal lore. They knew the smell of live oak and cedar smoke as I do, the taste of venison and limestone water and native pecans, the feel of the seasons' change, the right uses of various woods, the calls of plover and geese overhead and a thousand other sounds that I hear too. But the bulk of their deep knowledge was lost, and I cannot learn it on my own.

This much I can feel about them. It isn't a lot but it's something, and I'm glad such men were here, glad to have from time to time a sense of their ancient, intimate presence on this land I now inhabit.

****

I'd have much more sense of that presence if someone had published a clear, helpful, honest book on what can be known concerning my local red ghosts and how to set about knowing it, a book of the caliber of this volume Professor Thomas R. Hester has given us about the prehistory of South Texas and the methods by which it may be pursued. In fact I do already know more about these things after reading him, for much of the information and instruction he gives applies to my area too. Archaeology, rightly carried out as Dr. Hester has done it and as he wishes more other people would, is a path toward grasping at least some part of that lost lore one would like to share with the old ones. It substitutes as best it can for histories that were destroyed or never were written down. It pieces together old human ways of life, migrations, trade patterns, and climatic and other changes that in the far past distributed human ghosts everywhere. It can help bring them to life.

Because such study, to be effective, must be as intensely regional as its ancient subjects were, because it must be conducted slowly and carefully, with long patience, by skilled persons willing to accumulate and sort and classify huge quantities of bone and stone and clay and charcoal and other relic material from many spots, and only then to decide what all the evidence seems to say, it will likely be a long long time before very many specific New World regions will have solid books like this one to work with and from, in order that the store of knowledge may accumulate still further. Backward-looking South Texans are therefore lucky, I think, and so are we other backward-lookers who live somewhere nearby.

John Graves
June 1980

TABLE OF CONTENTS

Acknowledgments   xix
Introduction   1

1. **ARCHAEOLOGICAL FIELD METHODS**   7
    Sites and Site Survey   8
    Excavation   11
    Some Basic Considerations in Excavation   15
    Reporting the Excavation   23
    Dating Archaeological Finds   25

2. **CULTURAL AND ENVIRONMENTAL SETTING
    OF SOUTH TEXAS**   27
    Human Antiquity in the New World: 27
        Paleo-Indian, 28   Archaic, 29   Formative, 30
    Modern and Prehistoric Environments   31

3. **HISTORIC INDIANS OF SOUTH TEXAS**   38
    Coahuilteco   39
    Karankawa   48
    Tonkawa   51
    Other Hunting and Gathering Peoples   52
    Lipan Apache   53
    Comanche   54
    Other Intrusive Indian Groups   56

4. **PREHISTORIC SITES IN SOUTH TEXAS**   57
    Occupation Sites   57

Workshop Sites   64
Temporary or Auxiliary Sites   64
Kill-Sites   66
Isolated Finds and Caches   68
Isolated Burials   69
Cemeteries   73
Rock Art Sites   82
Rockshelter and Cave Sites   86

5. **MAJOR ARTIFACT TYPES OF SOUTH TEXAS**   87
Making Stone Tools   87
Projectile Points   94
Tools   108
Ground Stone Artifacts   115
Bone and Antler Artifacts   120
Shell Artifacts   120
Pottery   122
Exotic Artifacts   128

6. **11,000 YEARS OF SOUTH TEXAS PREHISTORY**   131
What is the Earliest Evidence in South Texas?   131
Paleo-Indian Period   134
Pre-Archaic Period   146
Archaic Period   149
Late Prehistoric Period   154
Historic Period   160

7. **PRESERVING SOUTH TEXAS PREHISTORY**   165

Appendices
    I.   Archaeological Societies in Texas   169
    II. Academic Programs in South Texas
         Archaeology   171
    III. Organization of Site Reports   173
    IV. Sample Record Forms   176
    V.   Journals and Monographs   180

References Cited   182
Further Reading   191
Index   198

LIST OF FIGURES AND TABLES

FIGURES

South Texas Site Map		4
1.1	Site Survey Record Form	9
1.2	Excavation Using Grid System	20
1.3	Hand Screens	20
1.4	Recording at Site in Northern Bexar County	20
1.5	Drawing a Profile at Site in Northern Bexar County	21
1.6	Column Sample	21
2.1	The South Texas-Northeastern Mexico Archaeological Area	33
2.2	Biotic Provinces of Texas	35
3.1	A Coahuilteco Indian of Southern Texas	41
3.2	A Karankawa Indian of the Southern Texas Coast	49
4.1	An Eroded Surface Site in South Texas	59
4.2	Excavations in Progress at Site in Zavala County	61
4.3	Excavation of Deeply Buried Occupations at Site in Live Oak County	62
4.4	A Burned Rock Midden in South Central Texas	65
4.5	Artifacts from the Bonfire Shelter Bison-Kill Site	67
4.6	Skillet Mountain Site: Kill and Butchering Locality	68
4.7	Bone Beads from Burial at a Zavala County Site	70
4.8	Isolated Burial at the Buckhorn Site (Dimmit County)	71
4.9	Examples of Burial Positions at the Floyd Morris Cemetery Site (Cameron County)	72

4.10 Artifacts from the Floyd Morris and Ayala
      Cemetery Sites   74
4.11 Burial 11 from the Floyd Morris Cemetery Site   75
4.12 Human Bone Artifacts from the South Texas Coast   76
4.13 The Oso Cemetery Site (Nueces County)   78
4.14 Burial at the Oso Cemetery Site   79
4.15 Bison Scapula Artifact   80
4.16 Burials at a Nueces County Site   81
4.17 The Loma Sandia Site (Live Oak County)   83
4.18 Rock Art Panel at Site (Webb County)   84
4.19 Baker Cave (Val Verde County)   85
5.1   Painted Pebble from a Site on the Nueces River   88
5.2   The Tool-Making Process   89
5.3   Flake Typology   91
5.4   Techniques of Stone Tool-Making   93
5.5   Using a Spearthrower   95
5.6   Sequence of Projectile Point Types   97
5.7   Major Dart Point Types   99
5.8   Major Dart Point Types   100
5.9   Major Dart Point Types   103
5.10 Major Arrow Point Types   104
5.11 Major Arrow Point Types   107
5.12 Chipped Stone Artifacts   109
5.13 Clear Fork Tools   111
5.14 Chipped Stone Artifacts   113
5.15 Hafted Scraper from Northeastern Mexico   113
5.16 Stone Pipes and Other Mortuary Offerings
      (Live Oak County)   116
5.17 Incised and Grooved Limestone Artifacts   118
5.18 Ground Stone Artifacts   119
5.19 Bone, Antler, and Pottery Artifacts   121
5.20 Shell Tools from the South Texas Coast   123
5.21 Bone-Tempered Pottery from South Texas   125
5.22 Goliad Ware Vessels from Karnes County   126
5.23 Vessel from Goliad County   127
5.24 Toltec Period Spindle Whorls from South Texas   129
6.1   Distribution of Clovis and Folsom Points in
      South Texas   133
6.2   Clovis and Folsom Points from Southern Texas   135
6.3   Excavation of Ice Age Mammals (Kenedy County)   137

6.4   Artifacts from Baker Cave (Val Verde County)   143
6.5   Artifacts from the San Isidro Site, Nuevo Leon   144
6.6   Paleo-Indian Projectile Points from South Texas   145
6.7   Major Sites of Late Paleo-Indian and Pre-
          Archaic Periods   148
6.8   Prehistoric Hearth at Chaparrosa Ranch   155
6.9   View of Excavations at Mission San Bernardo   161
6.10   Artifacts of Mission Indians   162
6.11   Locations of Spanish Colonial Missions
          and Settlements   163

TABLES

1.1   County Symbols for Archaeological Site
          Designation   12-13
2.1   Some Very General Time Perspectives   32
3.1   Names and Locations of Some Coahuilteco Groups   44
6.1   Plant Remains from the Golondrina Complex
          Hearth, Baker Cave   140
6.2   Faunal Remains Identified from Golondrina
          Complex Hearth, Baker Cave   141
6.3   General Chronologies for South Texas and
          Adjacent Areas   156

ACKNOWLEDGMENTS

There are many persons to acknowledge in this book. The dedication, to Wade House (Carrizo Springs) and T. C. Hill, Jr., (Crystal City), bespeaks my debt and gratitude to two outstanding amateur archaeologists of south Texas. Wade House for many years served as the mentor of the Carrizo Springs High School Archaeological Society; through his efforts, many students learned of the scientific merits of archaeology and at least two of his students (the writer included) went on to earn doctorates in anthropology. T. C. Hill, Jr., has worked with me on many projects and many publications in the last decade. His hard work, keen understanding of the prehistoric peoples behind the artifacts, and his enthusiasm have inspired me, as well as countless other persons interested in south Texas archaeology.

My wife, Lynda, and our daughters, Lesley and Amy, are to be especially thanked for their patience during the time I was busy on this book, and for the encouragement that permitted me to see it through to completion.

It was one of my grandmothers, Mrs. J. L. Hester, who first got me interested in Indian artifacts. Her support and encouragement, and that of my parents, Mr. and Mrs. J. T. Hester—who allowed their eldest son to roam the countryside in pursuit of what must have seemed a rather strange pastime—are all deeply acknowledged.

There are many other people to thank, and I am sure that some will be unintentionally missed. Jan Ferrari (San Antonio) drew many of the illustrations for this volume. Dr. Frank A. Weir (Austin) graciously allowed the use of his drawings in Chapter 3. I am grateful to many professional colleagues for their aid, both during the preparation of this book and in times past: at The University of Texas at San Antonio—Dr. Joel Gunn, Dr. R. E. W. Adams, Dr. Thomas C. Greaves, Jack D. Eaton, Anne A. Fox, Grant D. Hall, Thomas C. Kelly, and the office and field staff of the Center for Archaeological Research; at The University of Texas at Austin—Dr. Dee Ann Story, Dr. T. N. Campbell, Dr. E. Mott Davis, and Dr. Jeremiah F. Epstein; at Texas A&M University—Dr. Harry J. Shafer; and the late Dr. Robert F. Heizer, professor emeritus at the University of California, Berkeley. I also thank Charles Johnson II and Dr. Frank A. Weir of the Texas Department of Highways and

Public Transportation for their help. For information on south Texas vegetation, I would like to acknowledge Wayne Hamilton of the Department of Range Science, Texas A&M University.

Many avocational archaeologists have aided me in my studies in south Texas over the past fifteen years. Most are members of the Southern Texas Archaeological Association, and I hope that by expressing my thanks to the STAA, I will reach these individuals. I would particularly thank William W. Birmingham and E. H. Schmedlin (both of Victoria), Jimmy L. Mitchell (San Antonio), and Ed R. Mokry, Jr. (Corpus Christi), for their continuing support.

The following persons, agencies, and publishing firms have provided permission to reproduce certain illustrations and I am very grateful for their courtesy: Texas Archeological Research Laboratory (Austin); Texas Historical Commission (Austin; Curtis D. Tunnell, State Archaeologist); Texas Archeological Survey (Austin; Dr. David S. Dibble, Director); Texas Memorial Museum (Austin); Department of Anthropology, The University of Texas at Austin; Dr. Raymond Suhm (Texas A&I University); Mayfield Publishing Company (Palo Alto, California); and the Center for Archaeological Research, The University of Texas at San Antonio. The Water and Power Resources Service (formerly Bureau of Reclamation) graciously permitted the use of certain data from the UTSA Nueces River Project; Stephen Ireland and M. B. Voth of that agency's Amarillo office have been especially helpful.

Many landowners in south Texas are to be thanked for permitting archaeological work on their farms and ranches. For example, much of the information compiled in this book is derived from studies that I directed at Chaparrosa Ranch, Zavala County. I am very grateful to the owner of that ranch, Mr. Belton K. Johnson, for his support and cooperation.

The Southern Texas Archaeological Association provided permission to reprint excerpts from its publication on the Payaya Indians. It is also particularly pleasing to see the STAA continue to expand its role in exploring and preserving the archaeology of south Texas.

J. David Bowen and Alice Evett of Corona Publishing Company are to be thanked for their work in getting this book into print; David Bowen originated the plans for the volume and I hope he is pleased by the results.

INTRODUCTION

This book has been written as an introduction to the prehistory of southern Texas. I hope it will encourage appreciation of the ancient cultures of this region among students, amateurs, and those who are just beginning to be interested in the vanishing record of the earliest peoples who lived on this land.

Archaeology by its very nature is a destructive undertaking. Prehistoric remains, once disturbed or removed, can never be replaced. So I have begun with some advice on how to dig—if digging becomes essential. Following that, the reader will find a review of ancient environments, a discussion of the Historic Indians, and a full account of the prehistoric remains found in the region, with descriptions and illustrations that will help to identify archaeological specimens.

Since archaeology does not end with the unearthing of artifacts, this book is also designed to aid in better *understanding, recording,* and *preserving* the archaeological record. In a region such as south Texas, where archaeological resources are abundant, there is a great need for "citizen archaeologists." My experience over nearly twenty years has shown me that there is a tremendous interest in prehistoric cultures; if all this interest and energy could be harnessed, how much more rapidly the mysteries and problems of our region's archaeology could be solved! An example of such combined effort is the Southern Texas Archaeological Association (an organization that I will mention more than once in this book). The individual, however, is still the key to the unraveling of south Texas prehistory: the farmer, rancher, businessman, architect and engineer, oil field worker, deer hunter, vacationer, and hobbyist—all have a potentially vital part to play.

Much of what is said in this book will be addressed to the relic-collectors, in the hope that they will realize the scientific potential of their activities—and the havoc they can cause in the reckless pursuit of an enjoyable and seemingly harmless hobby. Having begun my archaeological career as a relic-collector and site-looter, I feel qualified to preach and to scold. I still shudder to think of the sites I helped to despoil in what was then the "fun" of artifact-hunting. Most professional and amateur archaeologists started out the same way. Somewhere along the line, one realizes that scientific contributions can be more rewarding than the accumulation of points in a cigar box.

The general public is often confused about the meaning of archaeology and about just what archaeologists do. To judge from newspapers and popular magazines, they are pith-helmeted, pick-wielding folk, interested only in spectacular discoveries—Egyptian tombs rich in gold, Maya temples, or the recovery of choice finds to put on display in museums.

On the other hand, the hobby of relic-collecting—whether the relics are chipped stone arrowheads or nineteenth-century bottles— is often called "archaeology." Individuals who have amassed large Indian artifact collections and display their arrowheads in exotic designs in picture frames are sometimes thought of as "archaeologists." Archaeology is usually considered an esoteric discipline, delving into the mysteries of the past: "*You're* an archaeologist? That must be very interesting. I always wanted to be one . . . ."

While it is true that archaeology and archaeologists can be linked to some of what I have just described, archaeology is a scientific endeavor which has specific aims and a set of methods designed to achieve these. It can be simply defined as the *anthropology of extinct cultures*, or, more commonly, as the *reconstruction of history prior to written records*.

Archaeology is a subdiscipline of anthropology. While anthropology is concerned with contemporary culture, archaeology seeks to shed light on cultures of the past. The dean of American archaeology, Gordon R. Willey of Harvard, has stated: "The objective of archaeology is the creation of an image of life within the limits of the residue available from the past." Or, as Frank Hole and Robert F. Heizer have put it, it is ". . . the study of the human past, particularly as it is revealed through material remains . . .". Brian Fagan, the author of many recent books on archaeology, calls archaeology

". . . the study of artifacts and human cultures, whether ancient or modern, by archaeological techniques . . . the systematic study of archaeological sites and the artifacts found in them as a means of reconstructing life in the past."

Archaeology is today a dynamic field of research. It pursues three specific goals: (1) reconstruction of culture history; (2) reconstruction of past lifeways; and (3) the study of cultural process. Within these three broad goals, many aspects of ancient human cultures are being studied. We have begun to unravel the social, political, and religious aspects of prehistoric life. We are examining the ways in which ancient peoples exploited the resources found within their environment, and how cultures successfully reacted to changes in that environment. Ancient patterns of settlement are being reconstructed.

In essence, archaeology is striving to look at the *people* of the past . . . the individuals represented by the artifacts lying in the dust. We must, of course, have a detailed knowledge of the artifacts, but our method of study must be one that enables us to look at the way of life these mute objects reflect. The archaeologist of today does not dig up *things*—he digs up "people." To have only a concern for the artifacts—the objects left behind by long-forgotten peoples— is a sterile pursuit. We have to keep in mind that these materials of vanished cultures were made by living people. The task of archaeology, then, as it is defined here, is to develop ways to reveal the lives and cultures of the peoples of the past.

It is my hope that this book will serve a variety of readers, who will want different things from it. For this reason, the same information may appear more than once, in different contexts. The occasional repetitions may be a minor vexation to those who read the entire book from front to back, but I hope that, together with the thorough index, they will make the book more useful as a source for research and reference.

Finally, the careful reader may notice that archaeology is sometimes spelled *archeology*. Archaeologists (archeologists?) cannot make up their minds as to how the term should be rendered. Archaeology is the preferred form in this book, but where others have used the second form, their preference has been preserved.

San Antonio
February, 1980

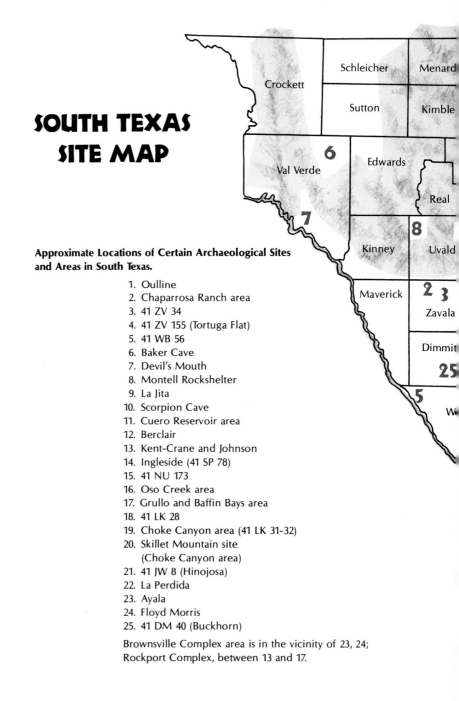

SOUTH TEXAS SITE MAP

Approximate Locations of Certain Archaeological Sites and Areas in South Texas.

 1. Oulline
 2. Chaparrosa Ranch area
 3. 41 ZV 34
 4. 41 ZV 155 (Tortuga Flat)
 5. 41 WB 56
 6. Baker Cave
 7. Devil's Mouth
 8. Montell Rockshelter
 9. La Jita
10. Scorpion Cave
11. Cuero Reservoir area
12. Berclair
13. Kent-Crane and Johnson
14. Ingleside (41 SP 78)
15. 41 NU 173
16. Oso Creek area
17. Grullo and Baffin Bays area
18. 41 LK 28
19. Choke Canyon area (41 LK 31-32)
20. Skillet Mountain site
     (Choke Canyon area)
21. 41 JW 8 (Hinojosa)
22. La Perdida
23. Ayala
24. Floyd Morris
25. 41 DM 40 (Buckhorn)

Brownsville Complex area is in the vicinity of 23, 24;
Rockport Complex, between 13 and 17.

Map 5

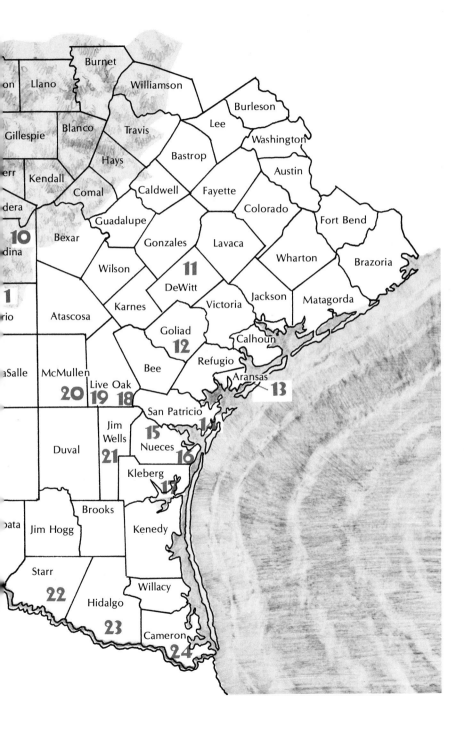

1
ARCHAEOLOGICAL FIELD METHODS

Archaeology focuses on the remains left behind by human populations. These materials may be *artifacts*—objects of stone, bone, antler, shell, or wood that have been modified or shaped by human hands. Or the remains may take the form of walls or structural remnants, rock art or cave paintings, burials, and the like.

Artifacts or other evidence of human activity are found at *sites*. A site can take many forms: earthworks, burial mounds, platforms or temple mounds, villages with houses that have left posthole patterns in the earth, villages with pit-houses, cliff dwellings; in the ancient civilizations there are pyramids, ceremonial and civic centers, temples, and cities.

In south Texas, the range is more limited. The following kinds are among those that have so far been encountered: *occupation sites* which were the scenes of everyday life; *burial* or *cemetery sites* where the dead were interred; *kill-sites* where the slaughter and butchering of mammoth, bison, or other animals took place; *rock art sites* with engraved designs (petroglyphs) or painted scenes (pictographs); *workshop sites,* usually areas of abundant flint where stone tools were made; *special activity sites* where a hunting party may have camped or a certain food-processing activity took place.

These prehistoric sites can often be hard to recognize. For historic times there are more distinctive remains—for example, ranch headquarters, Spanish missions, early settlers' cabins, trash dumps, and frontier forts.

SITES AND SITE SURVEY

The most common prehistoric sites in south Texas are the occupation sites, representing the camping activities of small groups of hunting and gathering peoples. Occupation sites are often linear areas close to and paralleling stream courses. Roving hunters and gatherers periodically returned to camp at these areas where water and food resources were known to be concentrated.

There are thousands of occupation sites of various time periods across southern Texas. How do we recognize them? Usually the surface is littered with flint flakes, burned rocks from cooking pits or hearths, broken chipped stone tools, scrapers, and projectile points. There will often be clusters of land snails (gathered as a dietary supplement) and mussel shells obtained from the muddy bottoms of the adjacent stream bed. If erosion has not been too severe, the cooking areas or hearths may be exposed intact as small oval areas of fire-cracked rock.

Occupation sites and other evidence of the prehistoric past in south Texas are commonly discovered during land-clearing for ranching or farming purposes, during plowing of fields, by the hunter walking through his deer lease, in road- or fence-building, in the development of housing subdivisions, or some other incidental fashion. The archaeologist usually finds sites through *site surveys*. These are systematic searches of stream drainages or other areas within which the ground surface is carefully searched for evidence of prehistoric or early historic activities. Site surveys can result from "contract" archaeology (surveys required by law before an area is disturbed), or they may be the focus of research by amateur or professional archaeologists, perhaps working through archaeological societies.

What is needed to conduct a site survey? First of all, the proper scientific approach is crucial. The survey is for the purpose of recording and properly collecting archaeological evidence; it is not an "arrowhead-collecting" expedition. Secondly, the permission of the landowner is required; jumping fences can get you into a lot of trouble and make a bad name for archaeologists. If the land is owned by the state or federal government, an antiquities permit (issued at the state level by the Texas Historical Commission in Austin) is essential.

I mentioned above that a "proper scientific approach" is necessary. This is not only a matter of attitude but also of methodology.

Fig. 1.1. A Standard Site Survey Record Form.

SITE SURVEY RECORD   Permanent No. _____

Field No. _____

Site Name_____

Date _____

Recorder_____ County _____

Map Name _____Map Coordinates_____

Location _____

Description of site:

Size_____Shape_____Type_____

Nature of Archaeological Evidence _____

Features_____

Vegetation_____

Soils_____

Topography_____

Present Condition_____

Name and address of owner _____

Activities of Recorder at Site (describe the nature of the investigations, what was done and methods used)

_____

_____

Materials from Site (list artifacts and other materials collected or observed at site; sketches should be made on another sheet)

_____

Number of Bags_____No Collection Made _____

Photographic Records:

Black and White_____Color _____

Recommendations:

Disposition of notes and collections_____

_____

Site surveys, like excavation (which is discussed later), should have a rationale and a goal. The rationale may be simple: examining a part of a drainage or an area of a county in which sites have not previously been recorded. Methodologically, the survey should adhere to strict recording and collecting techniques. A consistent approach should be taken in filling out *site survey forms* (Fig. 1.1) and plotting the site locations on the best available maps. (Usually these are the topographic sheets of the U.S. Geological Survey.) Unless the site is in imminent danger of destruction or is subject to intensive relic-hunting, collecting should be limited and carefully controlled. If points and tools are collected from the site surface, their locations should be plotted on a measured sketch map of the site. Similar plottings should be done of hearth areas, snail shell or mussel shell concentrations, or other cultural features which are observed.

Forms such as the one shown in Fig. 1.1 are convenient, but they should not be a substitute for *thinking* about the site. Filling in a site survey form will provide basic information, but thinking and asking questions about the site will usually lead to the recording of additional information which will greatly supplement the site survey form. Photographs—black and white or color slides—should be taken of each site (unless, of course, the site is covered in heavy brush with the resulting photograph simply a picture of mesquite trees!). A 35 mm camera is the best lightweight camera for site survey purposes, but a carefully framed snapshot with "instamatic" type cameras will also be of value.

The completed site survey form should be placed on permanent file with an institution responsible for keeping site records. You should retain a copy for your own files. In Texas, it is recommended that site survey forms be sent to the Texas Archeological Research Laboratory, Balcones Research Center, 10,000 Burnet Road, Austin, Texas 78758. While many universities and museums in the state maintain site record files, the laboratory at Balcones Research Center serves as the *central* state file. When your survey form is received, you will be sent an official, permanent site number. In Texas, site numbers are assigned utilizing a trinomial system first implemented by the Smithsonian Institution. The number might read: 41 BX 228. "41" represents the State of Texas in the Smithsonian's alphabetical list of the states; "BX" is the code for Bexar County; and "228" signifies that this is the 228th site to be officially recorded in Bexar County. (Throughout this book, the official site numbers will be given for various important sites. The county abbreviations used for Texas are listed in Table 1.1.)

Here is a list of some basic equipment that is needed for field work during a site survey:

Basic Equipment for Site Survey
Lightweight, easily usable camera; film
Paper or cloth sacks for collecting purposes
Tape measure: 6 foot or 2 meter, or 100 foot (30 meter) tapes
   are best
4- or 6- inch pointing trowel for exposing artifacts and features
Pocket compass for determining cardinal directions
   and map-making
Pencils for note-taking and marking pens for labeling sacks
Small entrenching shovel for emergency excavation
Ruler and protractor for map-making
Whisk broom and paint brush for clearing features
Photographic scale to be used in photographs of site or features
   (a scale made in the form of a directional arrow is most useful)
Notebook for holding record forms, graph paper, note paper
USGS topographic maps or county highway maps
Knapsack for carrying equipment

In addition to this archaeological equipment, a canteen, a good hat or cap, and a compact first-aid kit also come in handy.

EXCAVATION

In general, excavations should not be undertaken without professional supervision or group participation, as in the case of a project by a local archaeological society. There are reasons for this, a major one being that most non-professional archaeologists do not have the necessary background and training to excavate in a thorough manner.

It must be remembered that all excavation is in itself destructive, and it is therefore the job of the excavator to make a full record of any such effort. As the great British archaeologist Flinders Petrie once wrote, "No one has a moral right to open up sites without securing all that is found . . .".

Additionally, when excavations are made there are usually large amounts of cultural material, aside from artifacts, which must be

Table 1.1 County Symbols for Archaeological Site Designation: Texas (41)

Anderson ......AN	Colorado.......CD	Gillespie .... GL
Andrews ....AD	Comal .... CM	Glasscock ......GC
Angelina ....AG	Comanche ..... CJ	Goliad .... GD
Aransas .... AS	Concho CC	Gonzales ....GZ
Archer ....AR	Cooke .... CO	Gray ....GY
Armstrong..... AM	Coryell.........CV	Grayson .... GS
Atascosa .... AT	Cottle.......... CT	Gregg......... GG
Austin..........AU	Crane..........CR	Grimes........ GM
	Crockett CX	Guadalupe .... GU
Bailey .... BA	Crosby .... CB	
Bandera........BN	Culberson ......CU	Hale ....HA
Bastrop .... BP		Hall............ HL
Baylor.......... BY	Dallam ....DA	Hamilton ...... HM
Bee .... BE	Dallas .... DL	Hansford .... HF
Bell .... BL	Dawson .... DS	Hardeman......HX
Bexar .... BX	Deaf Smith ..... DF	Hardin .... HN
Blanco .... BC	Delta .... DT	Harris ....HR
Borden.........BD	Denton .... DN	Harrison .... HS
Bosque.........BQ	De Witt .... DW	Hartley......... HT
Bowie.......... BW	Dickens ....DK	Haskell.........HK
Brazoria........BO	Dimmit .... DM	Hays ....HY
Brazos .... BZ	Donley.........DY	Hemphill ...... HH
Brewster .... BS	Duval .... DV	Henderson ..... HE
Briscoe..........BI		Hidalgo .... HG
Brooks .... BK	Eastland .... EA	Hill .... HI
Brown .... BR	Ector........... EC	Hockley .... HQ
Burleson .... BU	Edwards........ ED	Hood .... HD
Burnet .... BT	Ellis ....EL	Hopkins........HP
	El Paso .... EP	Houston ...... HO
Caldwell ...... CW	Erath........... ER	Howard .... HW
Calhoun CL		Hudspeth ......HZ
Callahan ....CA	Falls .... FA	Hunt.......... HU
Cameron .... CF	Fannin .... FN	Hutchinson.....HC
Camp.......... CP	Fayette......... FY	
Carson .... CZ	Fisher...........FS	Irion ....IR
Cass .... CS	Floyd ....FL	
Castro ....CAS	Foard .... FD	Jack.............JA
Chambers ......CH	Fort Bend ...... FB	Jackson ....JK
Cherokee ...... CE	Franklin .... FK	Jasper...........JP
Childress CI	Freestone ...... FT	Jeff Davis ....JD
Clay ....CY	Frio .... FR	Jefferson ....JF
Cochran ...... CQ		Jim Hogg.......JH
Coke ....CK		Jim Wells ....JW
Coleman ....CN	Gaines ....GA	Johnson ....JN
Collin........ COL	Galveston ......GV	Jones ....JS
Collingsworth ..CG	Garza ....GR	

Karnes ....KA
Kaufman .... KF
Kendall .... KE
Kenedy ....KN
Kent .... KT
Kerr .... KR
Kimble .... KM
King ....KG
Kinney .... KY
Kleberg .... KL
Knox........... KX

Lamar .... LR
Lamb .... LA
Lampasas ....LM
La Salle ....LS
Lavaca LC
Lee ....LE
Leon........... LN
Liberty .... LB
Limestone ....LT
Lipscomb....... LP
Live Oak .... LK
Llano LL
Loving LV
Lubbock .... LU
Lynn ....LY

Madison ...... MA
Marion........ MR
Martin .... MT
Mason ....MS
Matagorda .... MG
Maverick ...... MV
McCulloch .... MK
McLennan......ML
McMullen ..... MC
Medina ....ME
Menard .... MN
Midland....... MD
Milam ....MM
Mills .... MI
Mitchell....... MH
Montague ..... MU
Montgomery ..MQ
Moore ....MO

Morris .... MX
Motley .... MY

Nacogdoches ...NA
Navarro ....NV
Newton .... NW
Nolan .... NL
Nueces........ NU

Ochiltree...... OC
Oldham........ OL
Orange .... OR

Palo Pinto ...... PP
Panola .... PN
Parker .... PR
Parmer........ PM
Pecos .... PC
Polk .... PK
Potter.......... PT
Presidio .... PS

Rains ....RA
Randall ....RD
Reagan.........RG
Real .... RE
Red River .....RR
Reeves .... RV
Refugio .... RF
Roberts .... RB
Robertson ......RT
Rockwall ..... RW
Runnels ....RN
Rusk ....RK

Sabine .... SB
San Augustine .. SA
San Jacinto ......SJ
San Patricio..... SP
San Saba ....SS
Schleicher.......SL
Scurry.......... SC
Shackelford .....SF
Shelby .... SY
Sherman .... SH
Smith ....SM
Somervell ...... SV

Starr .... SR
Stephens ....SE
Sterling .... ST
Stonewall....... SN
Sutton .... SU
Swisher ....SW

Tarrant .... TR
Taylor .... TA
Terrell.......... TE
Terry .... TY
Throckmorton .. TH
Titus .... TT
Tom Green ..... TG
Travis .... TV
Trinity.......... TN
Tyler .... TL

Upshur.........UR
Upton.......... UT
Uvalde ....UV

Val Verde.......VV
Van Zandt ......VN
Victoria .... VT

Walker .... WA
Waller..........WL
Ward.......... WR
Washington.... WT
Webb .... WB
Wharton ...... WH
Wheeler ....WE
Wichita .... WC
Wilbarger ..... WG
Willacy........ WY
Williamson ....WM
Wilson .... WN
Winkler .... WK
Wise ....WS
Wood .... WD

Yoakum .... YK
Young.......... YN

Zapata .... ZP
Zavala.......... ZV

washed, cataloged, reported, and stored. Again, most individuals do not have the facilities for such extensive follow-up.

Finally, excavation ought to be done only with specific problems in mind—scientifically-oriented problems which digging can help solve—and never solely for the recovery of artifacts. To dig up points and other artifacts simply to satisfy the collecting urge is the single most destructive activity affecting archaeological sites in Texas today.

There are times when the amateur archaeologist will have to carry out a limited excavation. A site may be threatened with destruction and no professional help may be available. In such a case, *test pits* ought to be excavated in the site to determine the age and cultural sequence, and to recover artifacts, faunal remains, and other cultural information. Or perhaps a local rancher has come across a burial eroding out of a gully wall or a farmer has plowed up a large hearth in his field and you are aware of the discovery. If you cannot get help from professional archaeologists or from fellow amateurs, you need to be prepared to undertake "salvage" work. Here your possible lack of training would be overshadowed by the need to rescue an important piece of prehistory before it is totally destroyed.

It is beyond the purpose of this book to provide detailed instructions for excavations, although some general guidelines are provided below. The serious amateur archaeologist should make an effort to build up his or her library with helpful books, and to get training by working with a local or state archaeological society. The most widely-used guide to archaeological field techniques is *Field Methods in Archaeology*, by Thomas R. Hester, the late Robert F. Heizer, and John A. Graham. The 408-page, 1975 revised edition is available for about $11.00 from Mayfield Publishing Company, 285 Hamilton Avenue, Palo Alto, California 94301.

Another recently published field methods book, also highly useful for the amateur archaeologist, is *A Guide to Basic Archaeological Field Procedures*, by K. R. Fladmark. Published in 1978, this book costs $8.00 and can be purchased from the Department of Archaeology, Simon Fraser University, Burnaby, British Columbia V5A 1S6. Some other less detailed or differently oriented books related to field methods are listed in "Further Reading" at the end of this book.

Basic Excavation Equipment
(See also list of Basic Equipment for Site Survey)
Long handled, round point No. 2 shovels

(square point No. 2 shovels can also be used at times)
4- or 6-inch steel pointing trowel
Tape measures (30 meter or 100 foot; 6 foot or 2 meters)
Paper or cloth collecting bags
 (paper sacks should be heavy-duty, #10 or #12 size)
Notebook and supply of forms (see Appendix IV)
Heavy-duty string and wooden stakes 1" x 2" x 24"
Sifting screens, with either 1/4" or 1/8" mesh
 (these should have legs or be rested on sawhorses)
Buckets, #8 or #10 size
Small tools: ice pick, whisk broom, paintbrush, dustpan,
 hammer or small sledge; line level
Camera and film
Aluminum foil (for charcoal samples); plastic bags
 (for small finds)
Pocket compass
Surveying equipment for site mapping (An inexpensive hand
 level and a stadia rod made by tacking a tape measure on a
 pole can suffice if transit, alidade, or other sophisticated
 equipment is not available —see Fig. 1.4)

SOME BASIC CONSIDERATIONS IN EXCAVATION

There are many excavation techniques, some designed for specific
kinds of sites or to solve certain kinds of scientifically-posed questions. But there are two basic rules in any excavation: (1) careful
observation and recording; (2) maintaining precise and consistent
controls.

First of all, you will want to document the *horizontal provenience*
or location of your excavation pit. The pit itself becomes part of
careful horizontal control and recordkeeping. If you can, select
a more or less permanent point on or adjacent to the site—a large
boulder, a telephone pole, a massive tree—and designate that (or
some point on it, created perhaps by driving a nail into the base of
a tree) as your *datum point*. This then becomes your primary reference point and you should key all measurements to it. This is crucial
because it allows future archaeologists, perhaps ten or twenty years
hence, to return to the site (or what may be left of it), find your datum
point, and key in your earlier research to any new excavation
program.

Using the datum point, you may want to lay out a *base line* (using either feet or meters; the metric system is most commonly used in modern archaeology) which ties in the area you plan to dig with the datum point. For convenience, base lines are generally oriented north-to-south. From the base line, you may then proceed to lay out excavation units, perhaps using a *grid system*. On the other hand, the grid system (Fig. 1.2) is usually employed for large scale excavations and your situation may require the lay-out of only one or two excavation units. Typically, archaeologists use square grid units, perhaps five feet on a side, or one or two meters square.

When laying out the unit, it is essential to keep it square, and this you can do by using your tape measure to lay out the unit in the proportions 3, 4, and 5, the last being the hypotenuse of a right-angled triangle. If you utilize a five-foot square, the hypotenuse will be 7.07 feet; a one-meter square will have a hypotenuse of 1.41 meters and a two-meter square, one of 2.82 meters. Thus you can drive in one stake, extend your tape measure five feet (or maybe two meters) in one direction, drive in the second stake, and then triangulate from these two stakes to drive in the third corner stake. The fourth stake can then be measured in. Usually a string is tied around the square to mark the edges and to help in recording materials found within it.

If you are excavating more than one square, you will need to give them individual designations. This can be simple: Unit 1, 2, 3 . . . or Unit A, B, C . . . If you have an extensive grid pattern laid out, you should designate the unit by the measured coordinates at its south-west corner. (For example, 20 meters north and 40 meters east of the datum would be expressed N20/E40.) In any case, laying out a grid in an accurate manner is time-consuming and usually requires the help of several people and the use of a transit or other surveying equipment (Fig. 1.4).

Excavation units do not have to be square; it is just that the square is usually most convenient. Needless to say, Indians never lived in five-foot squares. In excavating an isolated burial, a rectangular unit may be more useful. If, in digging your unit, you find something that lies just beyond one of the walls, you may want to add an extension to your unit in order to fully expose, record, and recover a particular feature. Whatever the shape of your excavation unit, it should be designed to give you control over your work and to make accurate measurements. Ragged, round holes are the trademark of the looter and relic-collector, not the archaeologist.

Within your excavation unit, you can use the pit walls (which should be kept neat and straight) and the corner stakes to record discoveries in terms of their *horizontal* location. Of equal importance is the *vertical* location of an artifact or feature—the depth at which it is found. Again, depending on the nature of the excavation, vertical provenience can be recorded in many ways. In Texas, where many occupation sites are not clearly stratified, *arbitrary* excavation levels are often used. You dig the unit according to preset arbitrary increments of perhaps three inches or six inches (or ten or fifteen cm). Starting at ground surface, remove all deposits down to the bottom of your arbitrary level. Zero to ten cm, for example, would be Level 1, ten to twenty cm would be Level 2, and so on. Depths of the levels can be measured along the walls of your unit from the ground surface, or by using a line level on a string tied to the base of one of your unit stakes; or, in a more extensive excavation, by a transit set up at your datum point.

It may be that during your excavation you will encounter *natural* levels; these, of course, have much more stratigraphic value as they represent actual occupational activities. A natural level may be a zone of concentrated burned rock, a soil layer discolored by heavy amounts of charcoal, or a layer of mussel shells. You should not confuse these natural stratigraphic occurrences with the soil changes which typify soil formation and development in the region. Whatever method you employ in recording vertical provenience, make sure you use it consistently and make certain that its purpose (as well as its end result) is to determine the vertical relationship of an artifact or feature in terms of other materials you may encounter in the excavation.

Each arbitrary or natural level that you dig within your unit must be treated in the following way. All excavated deposits must be screened or sifted (Fig. 1.3). All artifacts and cultural materials found within the level must be plotted and recorded on your record forms (see Appendix IV), and all these items, along with specimens found on the screen, have to be *bagged* according to level. The bag should be of sturdy paper or cloth (a heavy-duty #10 or #12 paper bag is ideal) and the bag should be clearly labeled, preferably with a marking pen, with such information as site name and number, excavation unit number or designation, level number (with the level depths in parentheses), name of the excavator and date. Level records and notes should be completed for every level, whether you found much or not (see Appendix IV for a sample of a level record form); do not proceed to the next level until you have finished the records for the one just completed. A scale drawing should be made of any features such as rock concentrations, snail accumulations, a hearth, etc., found within the level. The configuration of the feature should be shown, its horizontal and vertical position recorded, and, if possible, it should be photographed in both black and white and in color. (Remember to include a scale in every photograph.) If possible, fill out a *photographic record* and *feature report* (see Appendix IV) for the occurrence.

In your excavation, it is important that you make every effort to maximize the recovery of archaeological information. This means careful attention to the collection not only of artifacts but also of other materials. Screening (Fig. 1.3) helps in recovery. A 1/4" mesh screen is the maximum size that should be used (flakes and small artifacts can be lost through 1/2" mesh), and if your site is rich in animal bones and other small materials, a 1/8" window-screen mesh is best. All flakes and other chipped stone debris should be collected and bagged. Such specimens are highly significant in technological research.

Animal bones should be collected and either carefully wrapped or bagged separately in order to protect them from breakage. Bone analysis tells us not only what the aboriginal food sources were, but also gives clues as to the habitat and environment in which the ancient people lived.

Charcoal should be recovered; in place (*in situ*) samples are the best, but if that is not possible, pieces should be picked off the screen. Charcoal found in place should be collected with a clean trowel or knife blade and dropped into an aluminum foil container. While no serious contamination of charcoal samples is likely to result from contact with your hands, it is always best to try to minimize all potential sources of contamination which might affect the dating process. Good radiocarbon labs have chemical processes which will eliminate certain kinds of contamination. It is most important that the charcoal sample be securely wrapped in foil and its exact provenience (vertical and horizontal) and its associations (with a cultural zone or a specific artifact type) be recorded.

Snail shells can provide information on both diet and climate, particularly the latter. There are several major species in south Texas, reflecting terrestrial and aquatic habitats. Most can adapt to changes in their habitats and are thus not especially sensitive to climatic shifts. However, the presence or absence of certain species will be informative. In some sites, there are simply too many snails to permit total collection. You may want to limit your collecting efforts, but do so in a consistent fashion. For example, you may choose one excavation unit in which all snails would be collected from the screen for every level, top to bottom. Among the major shell species in the region are *Rabdotus* (formerly *Bulimulus*; the common land snail), *Helicina, Mesodon, Helisoma, Polygyra,* and *Practicollela*. There are others, particularly smaller species found in fine-screening. One kind of snail, a long, conical form, is known as *Rumina decollata*; it was introduced into south Texas from the Mediterranean during European colonization in the Historic era. It is a burrowing snail and is often found in the top one or two levels of an excavation unit in area sites.*

It is also of importance at many sites to take soil samples. These can provide the basis for pollen analysis, chemical studies of the soil, phytolith studies, and the constituent analysis of the site deposits. The best procedure is to take a column of samples which span the full range of the buried deposits (Fig. 1.6). For some sites, a sample ten cm on each side (10 cm^3) is sufficient; at others, a twenty cm^3 sample is better. If pollen recovery is difficult in your area, the larger the sample the better.

Unfortunately, pollen studies conducted to date by V. M. Bryant, Jr., and Phil Dering of Texas A&M University have indicated that pollen preservation is very poor at south Texas occupation sites. This is due to the nature of the soil and to fungal spores in the soil which destroy the pollen. It may be that with more refined techniques in the future, better pollen recovery will be possible in the region. Soil chemical analyses can help to determine the nature of human occupation, particularly phosphate analysis which detects soils that have been chemically enriched by human activities. Such tests can be conducted by the Texas A&M Soil Testing Laboratory

---

*More detailed information on identification, habitat preferences, and ecological implications of south Texas snails can be found in the paper by Allen and Cheatum (1960) or in a series of pamphlets issued by the Dallas Museum of Natural History, "The Aquatic and Land Mollusca of Texas", *Bulletin 1* (in three parts plus one supplement), by E. P. Cheatum, R. W. Fullington, and W. L. Pratt, Jr. These were published between 1971 and 1974 and cost $11.00 for the set (P. O. Box 26193, Dallas, Texas 75226).

Figure 1.2. **Example of Excavation Using the Grid System**. Site 41 LK 67, Live Oak County. Stakes have been set in a grid system based on one-meter squares. Note other aspects of the excavation process: screening, note-taking, and in the foreground, a transit for making precise measurements of distance and depth.

Figure 1.4 **Archaeological Recording at Site 41 BX 228**. Field workers are shown using a transit (left) and stadia rod (right) to record the elevation and depth of 5,000-6,000-year-old archaeological deposits at site 41 BX 228, northern Bexar County.

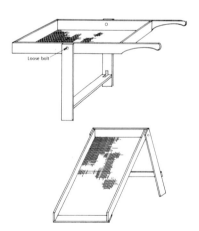

Figure 1.3 **Examples of Two Kinds of Hand Screens**. These screens, and larger ones that can be set on supports such as sawhorses, should be of 1/4″ or 1/8″ mesh. (Adapted from Hester, Heizer, and Graham 1975: Fig. 5.1.)

Figure 1.5 **Drawing a Profile at Site 41 BX 228, Bexar County.** Archaeologist on the right prepares a scale drawing of the excavated profile, while archaeologist on left aids by taking measurements and observations.

Figure 1.6 **A Column Sample Taken From Excavation Unit.** Site 41 ZV 83, Chaparrosa Ranch, Zavala County. Note soil sample bags in foreground; each is labeled with temporary site number, unit, and depth of sample.

and by the UTSA Center for Archaeological Research's Chemical Archaeology Laboratory.

Phytolith analysis involves the identification of plants from "opal phytoliths" or "biosilicas." These are microscopic plant residues that are—unlike pollen—incredibly resistant to destruction and that can be pinpointed not only to plant species but to a particular part of a plant! As this book is written, the most active program of phytolith research in the state is being conducted by Ralph Robinson, a research associate at the UTSA Center for Archaeological Research. Phytolith analysis is a slow, tedious study, requiring the resources of a chemical laboratory and an extensive type collection of phytoliths from modern plants for comparative purposes. (For a better idea as to what is involved in such research, see the 1979 monograph by Robinson.)

Constituent analysis of soil samples from a site helps to shed light on the nature of the deposits and how they were formed. Such studies are often called "matrix analysis", "constant volume analysis", or "midden constituent analysis." Much work in this area has been done with shell middens, where the deposits are almost totally composed of shells; the kinds and frequencies of shell species are important data in this regard. In occupation sites typical of the interior of south Texas, constituent analysis permits the archaeologist to look for charred seeds, to recover tiny snails, and to gauge the frequency of the distribution of burned rocks, flakes, and other debris in the site deposits.

For such studies, a consistently-taken vertical sample is important. This can be done by column samples as described above; UTSA archaeological teams use a "constant volume" approach, taking a sample of specific size (often twenty cm on a side) from a certain spot within each level, e.g., one of the corners of the unit. In the laboratory, such samples can be dry-screened or water-screened through fine-mesh geologic sieves, or flotation (often involving the addition of chemicals) can be done by immersing the samples, or portions thereof, in water and allowing the fine, light materials to come to the surface. In most cases, parts of a sample will first be extracted for pollen, phytolith, and chemical studies, and the rest subjected to fine screening and/or flotation for constituent analysis.

Of course, many of the special studies I have described in the preceding paragraphs can be done only by experts or by the archaeologist after long training and experience. What I hope the discussion has shown is that *all* of the site is a potential source of information, and that artifact recovery is only one small part.

It is crucial during any excavation that records and notes be kept as fully as possible. A neatly dug excavation unit with pretty, straight walls means little if you have not been making careful records and *thinking* about what you have been doing.

When the excavation unit has been completely dug (you have gone down to sterile soil or you have exposed the burial or other feature for which the unit was opened up), you need to make a scale drawing of one or more of the unit walls. This is called a *profile* and it is a valuable record of the stratigraphy you have exposed during excavations. With the drawing of a profile, you can record natural soil changes, the presence of natural or cultural zones, and other data pertinent to the interpretation of the unit and important to the meaning of your vertical controls. These "vertical" maps should be drawn with care and precision (see Fig. 1.5). Essential to drawing a good profile is a cleaned and scraped wall, thoughtful and careful delineation of exposed strata or items in the wall, and a clearly drawn record. You also need to record the colors of the soil changes. The colors should be based, if possible, on a standard color chart, such as the Munsell color chart (2441 North Calvert Street, Baltimore, Maryland 21218; $36.00) or the rock color chart of the Geological Society of America (3300 Penrose Place, Boulder, Colorado 80301; $8.00). The texture and composition of each strata should be recorded.

Finally, before backfilling your unit, you may want to take a *column sample* from the wall (see Fig. 1.6). These soil samples, noted earlier in this chapter, can later be of value to professional archaeologists doing research on sedimentology (as a clue to past geological processes) or attempting to recover pollen grains or plant phytoliths needed to interpret prehistoric vegetation and climate patterns.

REPORTING THE EXCAVATION

What do you do with the materials you have recovered from an excavation unit? First, they must be carefully washed and cleaned. Then they should be *cataloged*, labeling each clearly with India ink and recording on a *catalog sheet* (see Appendix IV) your description of each item. If you are not equipped or prepared to follow through on the materials that have been excavated, get in touch with a professional archaeologist, a local museum, or your local archaeological society to see if they will take over this important responsibility. As stressed earlier, you really should not undertake to dig unless you are willing to do the equally hard laboratory work that follows.

Cataloging and analysis of artifacts takes background, training, and access to some good basic references in your library. In Chapter 5 of this book there are some descriptions and illustrations of major categories of artifacts in southern Texas. These will help, but the ability to do accurate cataloging will necessitate contacts with professional archaeologists and participation in cataloging sessions in your local society. The need by amateurs to excavate and rescue materials is often a pressing one, done under the excitement of helping to salvage threatened information. After it is over, the staggering task of cataloging awaits the excavator! It is common, even in well-structured archaeological societies, to have fifty to sixty people show up to help with the excavation (it's fun!) but only a handful will come for the cataloging sessions after the dig is over.

Even more crucial in some ways than the cataloging and proper storage of your excavated artifacts and materials is the preparation of a report. The report may be simple and straightforward (although it should contain all the facts you so carefully recorded in the field) and might be designed as simply a letter report to be filed with a university research unit or a museum. If you have really been hooked by archaeology, you will want to do more. You will want to prepare a report (perhaps at first a preliminary report, to be followed by a final report after the cataloging and analysis is done) to be published in the local or state archaeological journal (see Appendix I). As described in Chapter 7, the Southern Texas Archaeological Association has an excellent and respected quarterly journal, and the editor is always willing to help you polish up your report in order to get it published. The Texas Archeological Society's annual *Bulletin*, usually 250-300 pages long, also seeks reports from amateurs (see Appendix I).

Having your work published is a gratifying reward for hard work in the field and laboratory; it brings you recognition from your fellow amateur and professional archaeologists, and most important of all, it permanently records the data that you have dug up. Unless you can prepare a report or, hopefully, a paper for publication on your digging activities, it is best never to put the shovel in the ground. Preparing the report is the most important aspect of archaeological inquiry.

DATING ARCHAEOLOGICAL FINDS

One of the most common questions asked by amateur archaeologists is, "How can I date my artifacts?" Radiocarbon dating is widely known, but many people erroneously assume that it can be used for all types of dating and that it provides very precise ages for sites and artifacts.

There are two general ways of dating archaeological materials: *relative* and *absolute*.* Relative dating allows us to gauge the antiquity of an artifact in relation to other artifacts; it does not tell us how old a specimen might be in calendar years. *Stratigraphy* is the best example of relative dating. If excavations have revealed a sequence of occupations (that is, a stratigraphic sequence), we can assume that those materials in the bottom zones are earliest, those in the middle come later, and so on. It is not always this simple, as artifacts can be moved around by rodent burrows or by the dynamic action of soils. The latter is a particular problem in south Texas, where some of our clayey soils—called "vertisols"—expand and contract, thus causing the displacement of materials buried within them (Duffield 1970). One can use relative dating with confidence only after a number of sites in a given area have been excavated, providing a broader picture of changes in cultural patterns and artifact styles through time.

Absolute dating permits us to determine the age of an occupation, site, or artifact form in terms of calendar years. Tree-ring dating (dendrochronology) is very accurate in this regard, but is applicable in North America only in the American Southwest, where one has the right kind of trees (pines), a distinctive growing season (to produce rings on a systematic basis) and the aboriginal use of the wood (as in roof beams in pueblo dwellings). It is interesting that one of the earliest demonstrations of tree-ring dating was by Jacob Kuechler, a resident of Fredericksburg in the 1840s. However, such dating cannot be applied in south Texas sites.

*The introductory archaeology volumes listed for further reading for this chapter usually provide detailed discussions of the various relative and absolute dating techniques. A particularly good review, written by R. F. Heizer, appears in Hester, Heizer, and Graham (1975: Chapter 14).

Radiocarbon dating can be—and has been—used for dating south Texas archaeological phenomena. However, several factors are necessary for radiocarbon analysis. The material to be dated has to be organic (or of organic derivation), there has to be enough of it (at least eight to twelve grams are needed), and it has to be in meaningful association with a cultural level, a specific artifact type, or something else that will give importance to the resulting date. Radiocarbon laboratories are swamped with requests for dates and you should be able to justify the reason for wanting your sample analyzed. Furthermore, radiocarbon dating is not cheap. Commercial laboratories will charge $200 or more for a single sample; university laboratories are often less expensive but they have more samples than they can handle. The university labs, therefore, carefully screen each sample and select only those which seem important.

A commonly used form of artifact-dating in south Texas is *cross-dating*. By this we mean a method of "comparative dating" which takes advantage of artifacts dated, by relative and absolute means, at sites in adjoining areas. In both central Texas and in the lower Pecos area, many sites have been extensively excavated, and relative dating by stratigraphy is available. In addition, a good number of the sites—and the sequences of occupations within them—have been radiocarbon-dated. We can determine, therefore, the ages of certain point types (see Chapter 4) in those areas. If the same types show up in south Texas sites, we can cross-date and feel fairly secure that we are dealing with artifacts of similar age.

2
CULTURAL AND ENVIRONMENTAL SETTING OF SOUTH TEXAS

Before examining the prehistoric archaeological record in south Texas, it is necessary to put it into perspective by examining the cultural and environmental setting—the human and geographical factors—as well as the Indian groups that occupied south Texas in the Historic period.

The cultural perspective permits us to compare archaeological findings in south Texas with the trends of cultural development recorded elsewhere in North America. With an examination of environmental factors, the resources available to the ancient peoples of south Texas are easier to understand.

HUMAN ANTIQUITY IN THE NEW WORLD

While it is widely accepted that man entered the New World via the Bering Straits (a "land bridge" at times during the Ice Age), there has been a vigorous debate among archaeologists about the antiquity of human populations in this hemisphere. Some sites—the Calico Hills locality in California's Mojave Desert is one—have yielded chipped stone objects for which claims of 40,000-100,000 years of age have been made. In the case of Calico Hills, these assertions have been rather convincingly dashed by C. Vance Haynes (University of Arizona); he demonstrated that the specimens are instead "geofacts"—rocks chipped and flaked by natural geologic processes.

In the past few years, a series of sites—the Old Crow River locality in the Yukon, Valsequillo Reservoir in Mexico, and Ayacucho in Peru, and a series of skeletal remains from southern California—have provided a little better evidence on the possible human occupation of the New World around 20,000 B.C. Still, this evidence is not as convincing as many archaeologists would like. The best data yet to be found for this early era comes from Meadowcroft Rockshelter, Pennsylvania, excavated by James Adovasio (University of Pittsburgh) and Joel D. Gunn (The University of Texas at San Antonio). A number of radiocarbon dates clustered at about 14,000 B.C. are associated with a group of definite chipped stone artifacts.

Paleo-Indian Period

The most secure evidence that we presently have of widespread early American Indian presence in North America is the Clovis Complex, radiocarbon-dated at 9200 B.C. The sites attributable to this cultural phase are primarily mammoth kill-sites, along with a few campsites, in Arizona, New Mexico, and the Texas Panhandle. Large fluted points, known as Clovis, are found associated with the slaughtered mammoths in the kill-sites. Following Clovis in time, we see a shift in the type of projectile point and also in the kinds of animals that were hunted. This is reflected in the Folsom Complex, with its smaller Folsom fluted points, found in kill-sites associated with now-extinct species of large, wide-horned bison. Folsom occupation sites, such as Lindenmeier in Colorado and the recently discovered site 41 BX 52 near San Antonio, have provided considerable insight into this early way of life around 8800 B.C.

Although some of the earlier archaeological literature and much of the popular literature refer to the Clovis and Folsom peoples as "big game hunters", there is now evidence that these populations used a wide range of food resources. Of course, the Clovis and Folsom hunters took their toll of mammoth and bison. Some scholars, like Paul S. Martin (University of Arizona), contend that these early peoples had a direct role in the extermination of certain animal species.

The peoples of the Clovis Complex, and probably those of the Folsom Complex, lived during the last part of the Pleistocene, or Ice Age, in North America. The climate and vegetation were radically different from what we have now. Temperatures were often much cooler, and forests and prairies covered many areas that are now desert. Most of the animals (like mammoth and the large bison already mentioned) were forms that are now extinct, including the American camel, a small type of horse, the ground sloth, various forms of antelope—all of which vanished with the end of the Ice Age.

Just when the Ice Age came to an end is not precisely known. It seems to have been rather gradual, perhaps covering a thousand years or more and affecting different parts of the hemisphere at various times. But by some time around 8000 B.C., the Pleistocene is gone, and climates, vegetation, and animal life become closely similar to those of today.

However, for another 2,000 years—until as late as 6000 B.C.—the life styles of the Early Americans did not radically change. This era (roughly 8000-6000 B.C.) is known as the "Late Paleo-Indian" period. Human populations increased and expanded into environmentally diverse regions throughout the New World.

Archaeologists often refer to the different Late Paleo-Indian cultures in terms of the distinctive projectile point types associated with each, including Plainview, Hell Gap, Scottsbluff, Meserve, Dalton, Midland, Angostura, and a number of others (see Chapters 5 and 6). Some of these groups hunted now-extinct forms of bison; others were oriented more towards plant food gathering and small game hunting.

Archaic Period

The term "Archaic" has been used to refer to the hunting and gathering, preagricultural Indian cultures of North America. We can recognize Archaic cultures beginning with the onset of essentially modern climates. In certain regions the Archaic began as early as 6000-7000 B.C., but was later in other areas. This cultural pattern continued until very late, even Historic, times in some sections of North America. However, in the Mississippi Valley, the Southwest, the East, and in Mexico, this way of life was later replaced by farming-oriented societies.

In the Archaic, food was obtained by hunting and gathering; in most cultures, the gathering of wild plant foods seems to have been predominant. There was extensive use of both chipped and polished stone tools (the latter particularly common in the Archaic of the eastern United States). There were chipped flint points and knives, and ground stone axes, weights, and ornaments. Bone, antler, and shell were used to make awls, needles, fishhooks, ornaments, and other artifacts. Some of the important polished and ground stone specimens include milling stones, pipes, and spearthrower weights (bannerstones, boatstones). In arid areas such as the Great Basin, great quantities of basketry, nets, and sandals have been preserved in rockshelter and cave sites. Pottery was not made. The bow and arrow was not known, and the spearthrower (*atlatl*), used in throwing short spears (often called "darts"), was the primary weapon.

Groups were organized as small bands, generally nomadic. Frequent moves were necessary in the food quest, and evidence of sturdy houses is generally lacking.

There was widespread regional cultural specialization in the Archaic; people were in every habitable niche of the New World and their cultures focused on the local resources. Along the Florida coast there was heavy exploitation of shellfish and large shellmounds are found. In the Desert West and parts of the Great Basin a "desert culture" was found in some sectors, while in others, like western Nevada, the Archaic peoples lived around desert lakes and relied on lake resources.

The woodlands of the eastern United States were rich in plant and animal foods, and by about 2000 B.C. there were sizable populations in that region, adapted to a relatively generous environment. The Northwest Pacific Coast area saw a development of technologies which served to exploit that region's rich marine life. A very sophisticated and elaborate society emerged, based mainly on fishing.

Formative Period

The development and spread of maize agriculture changed the Archaic lifeway in some areas. In central Mexico, farming developed out of hunting and gathering cultures as early as 5000 B.C. This started the development in that region toward the first civilizations of the New World, recognized about 2000 B.C. (such as the Olmec culture on the Mexican Gulf Coast) and culminating in the great prehispanic cultures of Mesoamerica—the Maya, Toltec, Zapotec, Aztec, and others.

Food production, pottery-making, and a settled way of life spread by diffusion into North America. The spread of this cultural pattern, often called the Formative, was slow and uneven. In the Ohio Valley, the Adena and Hopewell cultures show evidence of limited agriculture around 1000 B.C. Accompanying this new way of life were more elaborate rituals and religious activities—and a stratified society, with upper and lower classes.

In the American Southwest, the so-called Basketmaker culture began maize agriculture around the close of the pre-Christian era, this leading to the development of the Pueblo culture. Related cultures, such as the Mogollon and Hohokam, began farming perhaps as early as 1000 B.C., in the context of a desert-oriented hunting and gathering people known to archaeologists as the Cochise culture. The Hohokam was influenced by cultural developments in Mexico as early as 300 B.C.

In the middle Mississippi River Valley beginning around A.D. 500-600, there was an accelerated development of Formative culture. Large sites were established, with ceremonial architecture (including temple mounds arranged around plazas and other structures somewhat resembling those of Mexico), large populations (one town, known as Cahokia near present-day St. Louis, had a populace of 20,000), extensive trade contacts, a widespread ritual-religious complex known as the "Southern Cult", and craft specialization. The Mississippian was the peak of agriculturally-based cultural development north of Mexico.

As Table 2.1 indicates, the ancient peoples of south Texas shared in the Paleo-Indian and Archaic developments. In the time span of the so-called Formative, there were also some changes in south Texas, including the introduction of the bow and arrow and pottery-making. However, agriculture and a settled way of life were still unknown. This was also the case among hunters and gatherers in the Great Basin, in California, and in parts of the Plains. The term "Late Prehistoric" is often used in these cases to denote those peoples who made some changes from the Archaic tradition but who did not fully shift to a Formative lifeway.

MODERN AND PREHISTORIC ENVIRONMENTS

South Texas is often thought of as the "brush country"—a vast region of mesquite trees and thorny brush set in a hot, dry climate. For some parts of the area this characterization is applicable, but the environment was considerably different in prehistoric times.

The southern Texas-northeastern Mexico archaeological area (Fig. 2.1) encompasses a region whose northern edge is along and just south of the Edwards Plateau and extending south into adjacent portions of northeast Mexico. The south Texas sector, consisting of 22.5 million acres, is crossed by several major rivers—the Rio Grande, the Nueces, the Frio, the San Antonio, and the Guadalupe. This is often referred to as the "Rio Grande Plain" or the "South Texas Plains." Elevations range from near sea level along the coast to over 1,000 feet in the rolling hills of the interior.

In 1950, W. Frank Blair included most of south Texas and northeastern Mexico within his "Tamaulipan Biotic Province" (see Fig.

Table 2.1 Some Very General Time Perspectives

Epoch	Time	Old World	Egypt	Mesoamerica	Eastern North America	Southwestern North America	South Texas
Holocene (Recent)	1,000	Middle Ages		Late Post-Classic	Mississippian	Pueblo Sequence	Late Pre-Historic
	500		Arabs	Early Post-Classic			
	A.D. –0–	Roman Empire	Roman	Classic	Late Woodland (Hopewell)	Basket-maker	
	B.C.	Greek Empire	Ptolemaic	Classic			
			Persian Conquest				
	1,000	Iron Age	New Kingdom		Early Woodland (Adena)		
			Middle Kingdom				
	2,000	Bronze Age	Old Kingdom	Formative	Archaic	Desert Archaic	Archaic
	3,000		Predynastic	Archaic			
	10,000	Neolithic					
	35,000	Upper		Paleo-Indian	Paleo-Indian	Paleo-Indian (Clovis, Folsom)	Paleo-Indian (Clovis, Folsom)
Pleistocene	50,000	Middle	Paleolithic				
	1.5 mil. yr.	Lower Paleolithic					
Plio-cene	4.0 mil. yr.	Man in Africa					

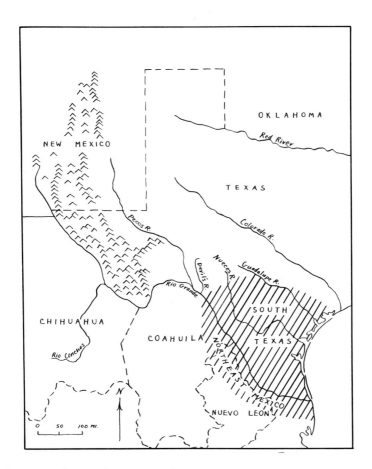

Figure 2.1 **The South Texas-Northeastern Mexico Archaeological Area.**

2.2). The climate is described as having high temperatures and low rainfall. Thorny brush dominates the vegetation in the interior; coastal marshes are dominated by sacahuiste grass. For most of the area there is a marked deficiency of moisture for plant growth.

Within the Tamaulipan Biotic Province, there is a wide range of animals; Blair's survey reveals 61 species of mammals, 36 species of snakes, 19 lizard species, and a few species of turtles and frogs.

Other authors have noted additional facts about the region's climate. Summers are hot and humid, with maximum rainfall in May and in September; winters are mild and dry, with lowest rainfall amounts recorded November-March. There is a pattern of decreasing precipitation from east to west across south Texas; on the east, annual rainfall is about 30 inches, in the central part, about 25 inches, and in the west, 20-22 inches.

In terms of natural vegetation, Shantz (1924) has defined three major zones. He describes the interior as a desert grass savannah dominated by mesquite. Along the Rio Grande drainage, he characterizes the vegetation as "southern desert shrub" dominated by creosote bush. A "prairie grassland" is defined for the coastal zone below Corpus Christi.

The widespread mesquite forests which choke the area today are a comparatively recent phenomenon, reflecting changes caused by ranching and farming since the nineteenth century. The spread of mesquite and thorn brush is probably the result of several factors. These include the commercial livestock industry (which led to overgrazing and the increased dispersal of mesquite seeds), short-term climatic changes, and the suppression of grass fires. The latter is especially interesting; some scholars have speculated that the end of aboriginal Indian burning of the prairies, as documented by the Spaniards (a practice continued by nineteenth-century settlers and ranchers), may have been one of the major causes of the spread of mesquite (Harris 1966). It is also interesting that present-day students of range management are reintroducing controlled brush-burning in south Texas as a way of regulating brushy growth.

Of course, we should not conjure up visions of broad expanses of grassy prairies completely free of mesquite. It is apparent from early Spanish records that mesquite was present, particularly in upland gravel areas and in scattered thickets along stream channels (see Inglis 1964). Work done by UTSA archaeologists near Three Rivers in Live Oak and McMullen Counties in 1978 indicates that mesquite was present along the Frio River as early as 1300 B.C. Still, as we will see, the vegetational patterns were apparently a far cry from those of today.

There was also more surface water available in the prehistoric period—at least in the last few centuries prior to European contact—than in modern times. Historic accounts confirm that the major rivers, creeks, and many smaller tributaries were flowing year-round. Many of the larger creeks carried water as late as the 1930s. But overgrazing and the resulting watershed destruction led to muddy runoffs that clogged the springs feeding these creeks. Coupled with this was the lowering of the water table in many parts of south Texas through intensive deep-well irrigation for farming. All of

Figure 2.2 **Biotic Provinces of Texas**. The south Texas-northeastern Mexico archaeological area is encompassed by the Tamaulipan Biotic Province. (Adapted from Blair 1950.)

these human agencies served to turn the streams into dusty chan-nels, carrying water only after heavy rainstorms.

In looking at the ancient environment of south Texas, it is obvious that we still lack sufficient information to make anything more than general statements. We know that the early Spanish explorers and Texan settlers found an area that was radically different, in terms of the distribution of mesquite and the presence of surface water, from what we now see. But how far back into prehistoric times can this pattern be extended?

In the closing millenia of the Ice Age—the Late Pleistocene—the south Texas environment has been described as a "parkland," with both grassland and forest elements. Mammoth, mastodon, and other now-extinct animal species were present; it was during this time, with cooler, moister climates, that humans first entered the region.

After the end of the Pleistocene, around 8000 B.C., the climate may have been one of gradually increasing aridity, a deduction we can make from pollen sequences from the adjacent lower Pecos River area. Ralph Robinson of UTSA is now getting indications of climatic and vegetational changes over the past 10,000 years through studies of plant phytoliths, the distinctive tiny residues which are left behind by most plants and are more durable than plant pollen. For instance, short grasses seem to have dominated the vegetation between 1000-3000 B.C., and tall grasses between 1000 B.C. and A.D. 1000. There are many other clues, based on his research, on geological studies, on the identification of charcoal as to wood species, etc. However, it is still too early for a coherent reconstruction.

We can safely picture a general environmental pattern with temperatures similar to those of today, with water more abundant and with vegetation more open—perhaps characterized in many areas as grassland savannahs. The uplands were probably more open, but with groves of mesquite and other trees; along the streams, there were concentrations of woody vegetation, as well as occasional mesquite thickets. It seems likely that all of the plants in the region today were there in the prehistoric past, but in differing numbers and varying distributions.

The animal life available to prehistoric Indians in south Texas was also different. There were bison, pronghorn antelope, bear, and prairie chicken. Antelope persisted on the coastal prairie through the nineteenth century; a few were still present in the interior (documented from Dimmit County) until just after the turn of the twentieth century. Bear occasionally still range into the region out of Mexico; a black bear was killed in LaSalle County in 1978! Bison were present in south Texas in varying numbers, probably on a cyclical basis according to research by Tom Dillehay (1974). There is archaeological evidence that bison were as far south as Alice (Jim Wells County), ranged through the interior, and were even present on the coastal prairie near Corpus Christi. Our best evidence comes between A.D. 1300-1800. Bison bones are found at earlier sites, but we still do not have enough information to establish any specific patterns.

There are animals present now that the Indians did not have available to hunt. The armadillo is a late intruder, not found in most of south Texas until the late 1800s. Javelina (peccary) was present in sparse numbers perhaps as early as A.D. 1300, based on materials from McMullen County, but did not increase in population until the 1800s.

In the prehistoric period, as in today's south Texas, some parts of the region had a higher density of resources than others. The presence of abundant resources (animals, plant foods, water) in one locale and the scattering of such resources in another would certainly have affected the way the prehistoric hunting and gathering peoples utilized the terrain, thus leading to differences in the kinds of archaeological remains left behind (Hester 1980). While the Spaniards reported that the Indians were often on the verge of starvation (see Chapter 3), this could not have been the norm. The variety of plant and animal foods in south Texas, some of which could be harvested in great quantities on a seasonal basis (prickly pear fruit, pecans, acorns), must have provided an ample diet for the ancient hunters and gatherers of south Texas.

3
HISTORIC INDIANS
OF SOUTH TEXAS

Comanche . . . Apache . . . These are the names that come to the minds of most people when Texas Indians are mentioned. What they do not realize is that these tribes were latecomers to the area, particularly in south Texas—moving into the region in the sixteenth and seventeenth centuries. The native Indians of south Texas and adjoining northeastern Mexico are less well-known. In the interior of south Texas, they have been called Coahuiltecan; on the coast, Karankawa. On the fringes of the Hill Country, Tonkawa peoples were probably present.

The sad truth is that we really have very little information on the native peoples of south Texas, and the prospect is that we never will. By whatever name they are called, these peoples followed a broadly similar way of life. They were hunters and gatherers, practicing no agriculture and possessing no domestic animals except in some cases dogs. They had no formal tribal organization, no dominant chiefs whose names have been preserved, and they left no mysterious ruins. Yet they are a fascinating people; they represent the culmination of more than *11,000 years* of a way of life that had successfully adapted to the climate and the resources of south Texas (see Chapter 6). We, as the descendants of European intruders, have been here—at the most—for less than *300 years*.

The prehistoric roots of the native south Texas Indians will be examined in later chapters. In order to obtain a better perspective, we first need to review briefly what is known about these peoples during the historic era.*

*It is not within the scope of this book to present detailed syntheses of the native groups. The reader should see W. W. Newcomb's *The Indians of Texas* (University

COAHUILTECO

The term "Coahuiltecan" was first used in the nineteenth century to refer to a language supposedly spoken by numerous hunting and gathering Indian groups in southern Texas and northeastern Mexico at the time of Spanish contact. In reality, there were no "Coahuiltecans" but rather dozens or even hundreds of independent small groups or bands of Indians who had similar lifeways. The Spanish recorded very little about these peoples; they were interested in "civilizing" them and in bringing Christianity to them through the mission system established in the region in the seventeenth and eighteenth centuries.

It has been determined in recent years, principally through the research of Professor Thomas N. Campbell (The University of Texas at Austin) and Dr. Ives Goddard (Smithsonian Institution) that some of the individual groups can be distinguished, that their approximate territories can be ascertained, and that other languages besides Coahuilteco ("Coahuiltecan") were spoken in the region. According to Goddard, there were seven major linguistic groups: Coahuilteco, Karankawa, Comecrudo, Cotoname, Solano, Tonkawa, and Aranama. There were likely others but information is too meagre to allow definition of these.

Campbell's research makes it clear just how little is specifically known about these peoples; for the most part, we simply have a name for a group (as recorded by the Spaniards), an occasional bit of information as to where they lived, and (more rarely) fragments of data about their lifestyles.*

Most previous studies, such as Newcomb's excellent book and a master's thesis prepared in 1955 by F. A. Ruecking, Jr., have made sweeping generalizations about the "Coahuiltecan" peoples of

of Texas Press, 1961 and a later paperback edition) for extensive descriptions of the Coahuiltecan, Karankawa, and Tonkawa groups, as well as the intrusive Comanche and Apache tribes.

*Much of Campbell's research is found in summaries prepared for the *Handbook of Texas*, Volume III (E. S. Branda, editor; Texas State Historical Commission, 1976). He has also prepared several studies of some of the groups, including the Payaya (Campbell 1975) who lived from southwest of San Antonio toward the Frio River, the Juanca (Campbell 1977), first recorded in the Frio County vicinity, and the Pacuache of the area of Zavala, Dimmit, Frio, and Webb counties (Campbell and Hester, MS). His monograph on the Indian groups present at the San Juan Bautista Mission Complex south of Piedras Negras represents most of what is known about the peoples of the Rio Grande between Eagle Pass and Laredo (Campbell 1979).

south Texas and northeast Mexico. These summaries probably depict the usual way of life of these hunters and gatherers. But the information is drawn from widely scattered early Spanish sources and deals with a variety of Indian groups from various spots in northern Mexico and south and central Texas. When these data are indiscriminately combined, the differences that probably existed (and which Campbell in fact found to exist) among the groups are obscured. Many of the groups were recorded by the Spanish after their lifeway had been at least partially disrupted by Apaches and Comanches invading from the north, or by pressure of the advancing Spanish frontier in northern Mexico.

The best information on the native peoples, in their natural state, is provided by the chronicle of Alvar Nuñez Cabeza de Vaca, a survivor of a Spanish shipwreck on the Texas coast in 1528 (see Covey 1972). However, Cabeza de Vaca's travels through Texas are the subject of much dispute. While it is obvious that he was among a number of the south Texas and northern Mexico Indian groups, we can identify only a few of them for certain. Historians and anthropologists have debated for many decades about the actual route of his travels, and it seems unlikely that this particular dispute will ever be resolved.

If we make *generalized* statements—and take them as such—about the "Coahuiltecans," the observations which follow are useful.

The Coahuilteco and other hunting and gathering Indians in southern Texas lived in small groups, each with a distinctive name and a territory utilized for the hunting, plant food gathering, and fishing necessary to obtain subsistence. They moved through their territories, sometimes overlapping into the territories of other groups, in a seminomadic fashion. More detailed population and territorial estimates are difficult, as many groups were often found in widely separated areas during the seventeenth and eighteenth centuries (see Table 3.1). Villages were established at favored locations near rivers or creeks, occupied for a short time, and then the group would move on.

We know very little about the numbers of people that might be found in these groups. Some have estimated an average of 145 people, but that seems a bit high. These higher population figures

Right, Figure 3.1. **A Coahuilteco Indian of Southern Texas**. Drawing by Frank A. Weir.

Table 3.1 Names and Locations of Some Coahuilteco Groups

These data are derived largely from summaries prepared by T. N. Campbell for the *Handbook of Texas*, Volume III (1976).

Name	Location or Territory (and approximate date of observation)
Aguastaya	Lower Medina River, south of San Antonio; early 1700s.
Atanaguaypacam	Mouth of Rio Grande on Gulf Coast bays and islands; mid-1700s.
Bobole	On or near the Rio Grande near Eagle Pass; northeast Coahuila; 1600s.
Cacaxtle	On the southward bend of the Nueces River in LaSalle and McMullen Counties; 1650s.
Cachopostale	On the Nueces and Frio Rivers between San Antonio and Eagle Pass.
Carrizo	Name applied to a number of Coahuilteco groups; below Laredo to Brownsville along the Rio Grande.
Chaguane	Between Eagle Pass and the Nueces River; late 1600s.
Chayopine	East of the Nueces River, near coast; Bee County area.
Coospacam	Lower Rio Grande between Camargo and Reynosa.
Garza	Among those included in Carrizo; near Mier as late as 1828.
Gueiquesale	Coahuila; crossed Rio Grande to hunt and gather wild plant foods.
Hape	Northeastern Coahuila; into south Texas for bison hunting.
Juanca	Between Eagle Pass and San Antonio; northwest Frio County, 1691.
Orejone	Bee County area was central part of their territory.
Paac	Between Nueces River and Rio Grande in the Eagle Pass area; Dimmit and Maverick Counties; late 1600s.
Pachal	Frio, Dimmit, Zavala Counties; 1690s.

Name	Location or Territory (and approximate date of observation)
Pachaque	Between Rio Sabinas and Rio Grande, northeastern Coahuila; 1675-1691.
Pacuache	South of Edwards Plateau between San Antonio and Eagle Pass; observed in Dimmit, Webb, Zavala, Frio Counties; sometimes ranged into northeastern Coahuila and to south edge of Edwards Plateau.
Paguan	Dimmit and LaSalle Counties; early 1700s.
Pajalat	South of San Antonio between the Frio and San Antonio Rivers.
Pajaseque	Near Corpus Christi; 1740s.
Pakawa	Nueces and Frio Rivers southwest of San Antonio.
Pampopa	On the Medina, Frio, and Nueces Rivers in Bexar, Medina, Frio, La Salle, and McMullen Counties; 1700s.
Pamoque	Mouth of Nueces River; Nueces and Corpus Christi Bays; early 1700s.
Papanac	Nueces and Frio Rivers to Rio Grande and into northeast Coahuila; 1600-1700s.
Pasnacan	Near coast; between the San Antonio and Nueces Rivers.
Pastaloca	Nueces River valley area northeast of Eagle Pass; late 1600s; Dimmit, Zavala, La Salle, Maverick, and Webb Counties; encamped in southern Maverick County in 1691.
Pataguo	Along Frio River in Frio County and in Dimmit and Zavala Counties in 1690s; earlier, ca. 1670, north of Monterrey.
Patzau	Dimmit and Zavala Counties and on Frio River; 1690-91.
Payaya	San Antonio area (Medina River) southward to Frio River; late 1600s.
Payuguan	Nueces and Frio Rivers between San Antonio and Eagle Pass; earlier, probably southeastern Coahuila.
Peupuetem	Coahuilteco(?); downstream from Rio Grande City; mid-1700s.
Piniquu	Both sides of the Rio Grande near Eagle Pass; 1700s.

Name	Location or Territory (and approximate date of observation)
Pitahay	Upper Frio River branches; 1690s.
Pitalac	Rio Grande upstream from Laredo.
Pulacuam	West of San Antonio, perhaps on upper Medina River.
Quem	Southern Maverick County, 1691.
Quepano	Near Cerralvo in northeastern Nuevo Leon; late 1600s.
Sampanal	50 miles north-northeast of Eagle Pass; also noted in the Nueces-Frio Rivers area; 1600s.
Siaguan	Reported on the Rio Sabinas in northeast Coahuila and also on the great bend of the Nueces River in Dimmit and Zavala Counties.
Sijame	Northeastern Coahuila; 1698.
Siupam	San Pedro Springs and San Antonio River; early 1700s.
Tamique	Near Victoria along Guadalupe River; early 1700s.
Tejon	South bank of Rio Grande near Reynosa.
Tetecore	North of Eagle Pass in 1700s and in Coahuila earlier.
Uscapem	East of Reynosa; also Cameron and Hidalgo Counties.
Venado	Duval County and into northeast Nuevo Leon near Cerralvo; 1700s.
Yeme	Laredo area in early 1800s; also included among groups known as Carrizo.
Yorica	Northeast Coahuila; late 1600s; hunted bison north of Eagle Pass (1675).

derive from Spanish reports of Coahuiltecan *rancherías*—villages comprised of several Coahuilteco groups drawn together because of the disruption of their usual lifeways. Probably there were fewer than one hundred persons in a Coahuilteco group most of the year.

They hunted a wide range of animals, including bison, whitetail deer, javelina, rabbits, rats, mice, and other small mammals. Snakes and lizards, terrapins, and other reptiles were hunted or gathered. Fishing was done by some groups; among others, the eating of fish may have been taboo. It is likely that the Coahuilteco, like most other hunters and gatherers around the world, based much of their subsistence on plant food gathering. The forested areas along the south Texas waterways provided an abundance of seasonally available plant foods, including wild fruits, nuts, berries, and seeds, such as those of the mesquite, oak, hackberry, persimmon, and pecan. Roots and leaves of agave or sotol, grass seeds, gourds, flowering weeds and plants were also harvested. Prickly pear *tunas* or fruits could be gathered in large numbers in the early summer. Some of the plants had medicinal qualities recognized by the Coahuiltecos; others, such as the mountain laurel and peyote, had narcotic properties.

The seasonal availability of the productive plant foods served to dictate the movements of some groups. When the prickly pear *tuna* were ripe in the summer, and acorns and pecans could be harvested in the fall, many groups would converge on areas where these plants could be found in abundance. Seasonal movements also were keyed to the presence of certain animals. Bison usually came into south Texas during the fall and winter. Some peoples from northeastern Coahuila would move to the Rio Grande at this time of the year to hunt bison and to fish.

Social organization was minimal; the family was the basic social unit. There were no tribes, no "chiefs" except those leaders that might be chosen for certain tasks because of their demonstrated ability. Little clothing was worn; capes and blankets were made of deer and rabbit skins. Houses were small brush- and hide-covered huts. Both polygamy and monogamy is found among their marriage practices. Certain rituals marked marriage, births, puberty, and death (see Ruecking 1954). Ritual cannibalism may have been practiced by some groups. It was a common practice among most North American Indians and, for that matter, hunters and gatherers in early civilizations in many parts of the world.

We know very little from the historic records about their material culture—the artifacts they made for utilitarian and ceremonial purposes. The bow and arrow was used, and they made curved wooden sticks for rabbit-hunting clubs. Nets of various kinds were used for hunting and fishing; baskets were made as containers and for food storage. Food was processed on stone grinding slabs (metates) and in wooden mortars. Hollowed-out gourds, the pouches formed by prickly pear nodes, and even human skull caps were used as containers and vessels. Pottery was being made or obtained through trade by some of the groups; others apparently did not use pottery until after it was introduced to them by the Spanish.

Communal activities were few. Groups would get together, as noted earlier, for seasonal plant food harvests. Some hunting might have been done communally by a group or by several groups. Ceremonies might be shared by several groups in time of war, or for cult activities or ritual dances.

Some anthropologists, relying on Spanish accounts, have written that the Coahuiltecos were always on the verge of starvation. Given the resource potential of much of south Texas (see Chapter 2), this could hardly have been a common state of affairs. Certainly it was a way of life that had few frills.

We can get away from generalized observations in only a few cases. The best documented group is the Payaya who lived southwest of San Antonio. After arduous research, Campbell was able to put together only twenty-six pages on this group. Following is his description of the Payaya way of life:

. . . the documents which record observations of Payaya settlements during the period 1688-1717 reveal disappointingly little descriptive detail on the aboriginal Payaya culture. Such information as is available will be summarized here and amplified by inferences made from other data considered to be pertinent.

The Payaya were unquestionably a hunting and gathering people who lived only in temporary settlements. Some of their encampments were unshared, but others were shared with individuals and families from one or more other distinctively named groups. Reports of unshared encampments need to be cross-checked for reliability whenever possible, for a single report of an unshared encampment is not as convincing as several such reports, and each case is strengthened when there is agreement between the reports of two observers of the same encampment on the same occasion.

We know nothing specific about the length of time any Payaya encampment was occupied before being abandoned, or its population size, or the internal space allocations when Payaya and non-Payaya shared the same camp. Nor do we have any satisfactory information on housing, such as house type and form, construction materials, and number of families or individuals commonly associated with a single housing unit. The records do indicate that Payaya encampments were near a water supply (springs and streams) and also near a wood supply (natural open spaces in a wooded area). Use of nuts from pecan trees evidently drew encampments to certain stream valleys in autumn, when nuts were harvestable. Salinas Varona (1693) recorded three Payaya settlements which were simultaneously occupied in early July and which seem to have been irregularly distributed along his travel route for a distance of less than 25 miles, thus providing at least some impression of settlement density in summer. Another source refers to a Payaya encampment close enough to a Pampopa encampment for exchange of visits.

Although the earlier documents never actually mention the Payaya hunting specific animals, they frequently refer to the abundance of game in the area, especially bison, and in precisely the same localities where Payaya settlements were encountered between 1690 and 1709. For example, in 1691 Mazanet repeatedly recorded bison seen along the route of the Terán expedition. On June 11, after crossing Hondo Creek above its junction with the Frio River and reaching the headwater tributaries of San Miguel Creek, he wrote that "on this day there were a great number of buffaloes and deer." The next day, June 12, in the general vicinity of the Medina River he reported ". . . a beautiful prairie where there were great numbers of buffaloes and deer." Then on June 13, shortly before arriving at the Payaya encampment on the San Antonio River: "On this day there were so many buffaloes that the horses stampeded and forty ran away." Mazanet continued to refer to frequency of the same game along the route northeast of San Antonio. This circumstantial evidence makes it difficult to avoid the conclusion that the Payaya must have made use of bison for food and artifacts when the animals were available. Later sources . . . indicate or imply bison hunting by Payaya in the grasslands between the Colorado and Brazos rivers northeast of San Antonio, and the processing of bison hides is also mentioned.

The only Payaya food-gathering activity specified in the documents is collecting nuts from pecan trees. This was recorded by Espinosa in 1709 in connection with his observation of a Payaya encampment on the Medina River. He referred to the abundance of pecan trees along the river and stated that the nuts provided a common foodstuff for all the Indians who at times encamped along its course. Later in the same document . . . Espinosa described the resources of the entire region traversed (Rio Grande to Colorado River) and presented informative details on the pecan and its uses. As at least one-half of his route lay within the maximum known Payaya territorial range, it can be safely inferred that what he says applies to the Payaya. Espinosa's brief, generalized statement is an important source of information on the probable role of the pecan in the subsistence patterns of various indigenous groups in southern Texas.

. . . According to Espinosa, the Indians of the area gathered pecans in great quantities. Some of the nuts were shelled and eaten shortly after being collected, but large amounts were also stored, evidently unshelled, in underground pits of unspecified sizes. Espinosa says that pecans were used for food the greater part of each year and also that some were consumed the following year. This may reflect the well-known fact that pecan trees in a given locality, because of variations in spring frost timing, do not have uniform yields every year. The implication is that the Indians may have been aware of this and stored more nuts in years of heavier yield, anticipating a possible lighter yield the next year.

These Indians were said to be skilled in removal of the nut shells without breaking the paired nut meats. If such nut meats were not eaten at once, they were not stored but temporarily contained in two different ways. The meats were placed in small skin bags or pouches or, less commonly, perforated and then threaded on long pieces of string. Although Espinosa does not so indicate, these methods of containing small amounts of a rich, concentrated food are very compatible with travel.*

KARANKAWA

The Karankawa are among the most maligned Indian groups of Texas. They have been the subject of considerable uninformed yellow journalism and the topic of ill-researched and poorly titled books. And they have not deserved these smear tactics.

They are generally thought of as "cannibals", and somewhere along the line they have also been classified as a tribe of "giants." They were neither.

The Karankawa were actually composed of a series of Indian groups who lived in the coastal strip from the Galveston Bay area

*Excerpted from pp. 17-19 of Campbell (1975), courtesy of the author and the Southern Texas Archaeological Association.

Right, Figure 3.2. **A Karankawa Indian of the Southern Texas Coast**. Drawing by Frank A. Weir.

south to the vicinity of Corpus Christi. The core of their territory seems to have been from Matagorda Bay to Corpus Christi Bay. (According to T. N. Campbell, the boundary zone between the Karankawa and the Coahuilteco was in the San Antonio-Nueces Rivers area.)

Theirs, too, was a hunting and gathering lifeway. On the coastal prairies they hunted bison, pronghorn antelope, deer, bear, and smaller mammals. From the waters of the bays and the Gulf, they took fish, oysters and other shellfish, turtles, and ducks. They often used narrow dugout canoes in hunting and fishing. Alligators were hunted for food, and the grease may have been applied to the body to repel mosquitoes. As a part of their subsistence activities, some groups moved between the offshore barrier islands and the mainland on a seasonal basis.

With two exceptions, Karankawa material culture differed little from the nearby Coahuilteco groups: (1) they used marine shells for making tools and ornaments, and (2) they manufactured a distinctive thin-walled pottery which they decorated with asphaltum (a natural asphalt which washed ashore on the beaches). The bow and arrow was the principal weapon. The Karankawa bow is often described as very long and powerful. The arrows were tipped with flint points and, after the arrival of Europeans, occasionally with points made of glass.

Their social organization was also similar to the Coahuiltecos. They lived in small groups or bands, perhaps of only thirty to forty people. They utilized a smoke-signal system to bring groups together for war or ceremonies—such as the *mitote* dance.

Cabeza de Vaca and his Spanish companions in the Narváez expedition found themselves among the Karankawa (or peoples related to the Karankawa tradition) when shipwrecked on the Texas coast in 1528. Reportedly, the Karankawa were friendly at that time, but this attitude changed to a warlike one after later contacts with the Spaniards, French, and early nineteenth-century Americans.

As to cannibalism, it was the Karankawa who were shocked by the sight of the starving Spaniards of the Narváez expedition eating the dead of their own party. As with some Coahuilteco groups, Karankawa cannibalism was ritual or magical in its purpose; vengeance was also a factor. In 1830, the botanist Jean Louis Berlandier during his explorations in Texas wrote of the Karankawa: "... Vengeance cannot be appeased save by actual cannibalism, a practice in which these people do not generally engage. This is why, in their summons to wars of revenge against the enemy, they say 'Let us go and eat this nation.'" (Berlandier 1969:77).

W. W. Newcomb (1961:78) has succinctly summarized the distorted image of the Karankawa: "Some of the atrocities attributed to these Indians are undoubtedly rationalizations growing out of the in-human, unfair treatment the Spaniards and Texans accorded them. It is much easier to slaughter men and appropriate their land if you can convince yourself that they are despicable, inferior, barely human creatures."

TONKAWA

The other native peoples who lived on the fringes of the southern Texas region were the Tonkawa. In the early historic period, the Spanish often recorded identifiable Tonkawan groups ranging into south Texas to hunt bison. There are major sub-groups of the Ton-kawa, including the Mayeye, the Yojuane, and the Ervipiame. The latter were apparently Coahuilteco-speakers living in northeastern Coahuila; they appeared in south central and central Texas in the early 1700s and later became associated with the Tonkawa. These groups never considered themselves part of a "Tonkawa tribe" until the late 1700s, after their numbers had been drastically reduced and they were forced together in order to survive. They persisted in central Texas into the 1850s. In January 1846 a group of Tonkawa rode into Corpus Christi during the time the United States Army of Occupation was preparing its invasion of Mexico.

The Tonkawa groups have sometimes been described as having a way of life somewhat similar to that of the Plains Indians. While they hunted and gathered many of the small animals and plants exploited by the Coahuilteco peoples, they apparently placed more of an emphasis on bison-hunting. And like the Plains Indians, they utilized the various parts of the animal—the fat, meat, hides, hoofs, bones—to the fullest. It is possible that some Tonkawa groups, or at least their Late Prehistoric predecessors, practiced limited cultivation of maize. Small cobs of maize have been found at some sites, dating to around A.D. 1300-1500; one such site is Timmeron Rockshelter excavated by the Southern Texas Archaeological Association in Hays County.

The Tonkawa remnants were eventually moved into the Oklahoma Indian Territory in 1859. As of 1964, one source reported that there were ninety-one left, and of those only four were full-blooded Tonkawa (Kelley 1971:164).*

OTHER HUNTING AND GATHERING PEOPLES

I have focused here on the Coahuilteco, Karankawa, and Tonkawa as they are the best known of the major linguistic groups of the south Texas area. However, as I noted earlier, research by Ives Goddard suggests four other major groups: the Comecrudo, Cotoname, Solano, and Aranama.

The Comecrudo are often linked with the Coahuilteco and it is certain they were quite similar culturally. They lived in northern Tamaulipas in the late 1600s and the early 1700s. By 1750 most were near Reynosa, south of the Rio Grande.

The Cotoname reflect a very similar situation and some anthropologists would also place them among the Coahuilteco, but Goddard believes they were linguistically distinct. They ranged on both sides of the Rio Grande in the vicinity of Camargo and Rio Grande City. It is reported that as late as 1886 some Cotoname were living at La Noria Ranch in southern Hidalgo County and at a locality called Las Prietas in northern Tamaulipas. It was at that time that A. S. Gatschet, an ethnologist who also studied the Karankawa, was able to obtain some of their vocabulary.

The Solano language was recorded at Mission San Francisco Solano in 1703-1708 (near present-day Guerrero, Coahuila). It is possible that it represents the language of the Terocodame, thought by some to be Coahuilteco-speakers.

The Aranama lived along the lower Guadalupe and San Antonio Rivers near the south Texas coast. They too have been classified in the past as Coahuilteco-speakers. They were important in the coastal missions at Goliad, at Victoria, and at Refugio. Some Aranama survived until the early 1840s.

Although these four linguistic families are known, in addition to Coahuilteco, Karankawa, and Tonkawa, it is Goddard's opinion that many others probably existed but were never recorded. All of the peoples shared a similar hunting and gathering lifeway similar to what we know of the Coahuilteco. However, these data indicate that the south Texas-northeast Mexico region was far more diverse

*In addition to the summary provided by Newcomb, the reader is also referred to a study by A. F. Sjoberg (1953a) where additional details on the Tonkawa can be found.

linguistically than once thought, and that it was not solely "Coahuil-tecan."

LIPAN APACHE

The Lipan Apaches were an intrusive people in central and south Texas, pushed by the Comanches from their homeland in eastern Colorado and northeastern New Mexico out onto the High Plains of Texas. They moved southward and their presence in south Texas is well documented by the 1700s. They were a nomadic people linked to some degree to the Plains Indian lifeway of bison-hunting. Before they acquired horses and prior to being pushed south, they also practiced agriculture, growing corn, squash, beans, and tobac-co. After they were displaced, agriculture became relatively unim-portant in their subsistence regime.

There seem to have been about 3,000-5,000 Lipan in central and south central Texas in the 1700s. They were raiding the San Antonio area in the 1740s, and they controlled south Texas by 1775. The Lipan intrusion further disrupted the already disintegrating lifeways of the Coahuiltecos and other south Texas hunters and gatherers. These native people were thus caught in a vise, with the Spanish moving in from the south and the Lipan (and later the Comanche) coming down from the north.

In Texas and Coahuila, the Lipan hunted and gathered a wide range of food items. They hunted bison along the lower Nueces and Guadalupe Rivers. Deer were next in importance in their economy and antelope were also hunted. There is a record of their hunting javelina (peccary) in northern Coahuila; they used the horse in hunting the javelina as it was considered too dangerous to pursue this animal on foot. Other mammals (bear, rats, wild cattle) were sought, as was the wild turkey, although it is believed that the Lipan in general did not eat birds, especially waterfowl.

In their food-gathering they are known particularly for exploiting the sotol . . . digging up its bulb and baking it in earth ovens. Like other Indians in south Texas, the prickly pear *tuna* was also impor-tant to them, along with mesquite beans and pecans. Whenever a group remained at a locality for a few weeks or months, crops of maize would be planted, but they received little attention.

Their clothing was made from dressed animal skins. In fact, the Lipan often traded deer and bison pelts in such far-flung areas as Saltillo, Coahuila, and Victoria, south Texas. They made baskets and coated them with pitch to make them waterproof. It is not known if the Lipan made pottery.

The bow and arrow was their principal weapon, the arrows tipped with steel points and sometimes poisoned (or at least dipped in a substance that to the Lipan had "mystic power"). They carried spears and shields and obtained guns through trade and raiding.

Warfare was an important part of Lipan Apache life. It had to be. The Comanches and their allies tried for more than a century to eliminate the Lipan, and no mercy was shown on either side in their numerous encounters. Torture and ritual cannibalism resulted from the bitter feud between the Comanche and the Lipan.

The Lipan Apache ranged throughout south Texas and northeast Mexico in the nineteenth century, raiding Mexican and later Texan settlements on the frontier. They struck deep into the lower Rio Grande area in the 1830s. While these hostilities are well known, it is also documented that the Lipan would engage in peaceful contacts, such as trade with the settlers. Indeed, a group visited the Army of Occupation at Corpus Christi in September 1845. But their raids, along with those of other scattered Apache groups, continued in south Texas well into the 1870s.

We are unable to recognize any distinctive archaeological materials of the Lipan Apache or to be certain of the identification of their campsites during the 1700s. Only at Mission San Lorenzo de la Santa Cruz in Real County are we positive we are looking at materials related to the Lipan Apache. This mission was built for them and operated between 1762-1771 (see Tunnell and Newcomb 1969).*

COMANCHE

There is a vast literature available to the reader on the Comanche, including Newcomb's (1961) summary, the book-length studies of Wallace and Hoebel (1952) and Fehrenbach (1974), and other literature listed in the "References Cited."

As Newcomb (1961:155) has said, "To many Texans the word *Comanche* is synonymous with *Indian* . . .". Indeed, the general public often links archaeological specimens from prehistoric sites to "Comanche battles" or other activities related to that tribe. In

---

*In addition to the summary of the Lipan Apache prepared by Newcomb (1961), the reader is also referred to Sjoberg (1953b), Berlandier (1969), Ruiz (1972), and Myres (1971).

reality, the Comanches came into Texas after the beginning of the Historic era. They were originally hunters and gatherers in the northwestern Plains as late as the seventeenth century, at which time they began to obtain horses. In the early 1700s they moved out onto the Plains, and by the middle of the eighteenth century they had become militaristic horse-nomads who controlled most of the southern Plains. Their expansion, as noted earlier, forced the Lipan Apache into central and south Texas. However, they were never a unified "tribe," but were rather about a dozen bands of different sizes, occupying separate territories. The Penateka Comanches were the largest of these bands and were the most active in the southern Plains area.

Comanches raided extensively into southern Texas, beginning in the early nineteenth century. Some towns, such as the settlement of Palafox on the Rio Grande in Webb County, were destroyed; Palafox had to be abandoned between 1818-1826 because of the continuing Comanche threat. Their raids and those of the Lipan Apache were particularly bad in south Texas in 1836-1837 when Indians traveled as far south as Matamoros. The Comanches kept up their raiding in south Texas until the mid-1870s. Accounts from the Dimmit, Zavala, and Maverick Counties region reflect raids by Comanches in groups up to two hundred strong in 1866 (a raid near Carrizo Springs in which one person was wounded with a steel-tipped arrow), in 1870, 1872, 1874, and in 1876, the last recorded Indian fight in the region. This one was not definitely linked to the Comanche. In fact, most of the accounts of "Indian fights" in south and southwest Texas in the 1850-1870s are unable to pinpoint the identity of the Indian group involved—it is simply "the Indians" (Fenley 1957).

Because of the highly mobile nature of the Comanche groups in south Texas, it has been impossible up to the present to identify the archaeological remains of any of their sites. Occasionally, metal arrow points (see Fig. 5.11) are found and some may be linked to the Comanches; on the other hand, such points could have been used by any of the other Indian groups that ranged through the region in the Historic era. In west Texas and in the Texas Panhandle, a number of isolated burials, placed in small caves or niches high in canyon walls, have been documented. Associated with them are various artifacts—knives, pistols, distinctive beadwork, horse trappings, ornaments, etc.—which have permitted their identification as

Comanche. (See Word and Fox 1975 for a review of the available information on such Historic burials.)

OTHER INTRUSIVE INDIAN GROUPS

There were other Plains Indians or southwestern Indian groups known to have been present in south Texas in the eighteenth and nineteenth centuries, principally as raiding parties. These included the Kiowa, Kiowa-Apache, and the Mescalero Apache. Cherokee, Delaware, Caddo, Seminole, and other displaced peoples from the southeastern United States also passed through the area at various times. A group of Pawnee paid a peaceful visit to San Antonio in 1795.

There is another Indian group that entered south Texas in the nineteenth century and whose descendants, now living at Muzquiz in Coahuila, occasionally return to the area as agricultural workers. These are the Kickapoo, a tribe whose homeland was once the Great Lakes area in lower Michigan and western Wisconsin. In the early nineteenth century the Indian policies of the United States exerted pressures which forced the Kickapoo to begin migrating west of the Mississippi, with many of them coming to what is now Texas. In the 1840s some Kickapoo, along with Seminoles and former slaves who had associated themselves with the Seminole, were living near Eagle Pass. In 1850 they negotiated an agreement with the Mexican government. They would help to protect the Mexican settlers against the raids of the Comanches and Lipan Apaches in return for land in the area of present-day Muzquiz. In the 1860s and 1870s, the Mexican Kickapoos were accused of raids into south and southwest Texas. This period of hostility culminated in 1873 with a raid by Col. Ranald Mackenzie and the U.S. Fourth Cavalry from Fort Clark (at present-day Brackettville) on a Kickapoo village near Remolino, Coahuila. Some captured Kickapoo were taken to San Antonio. However, the Kickapoo continued their raids on Texas and their fights with Apache groups in the region. In 1883 a Kickapoo reservation was established in the Indian Territory (now Oklahoma), and several hundred Kickapoo eventually settled there, although constant contacts were kept with the larger population at Muzquiz.*

*The Kickapoo still maintain many of their ancient traditions, their language, and a dual Mexican and American citizenship. They are the subject of books by Felipe and Dolores LaTorre (1976) and A. M. Gibson (1963) and a good summary article by Goggin (1951).

4
PREHISTORIC SITES
IN SOUTH TEXAS

There are a variety of archaeological sites in south Texas. This chapter describes the important types and notes some specific examples. As a guide to the reader seeking details, there are included a number of references to articles and monographs dealing with them.

OCCUPATION SITES

The place where daily living took place—the campsite—is the most common of all prehistoric sites in south Texas. Creek banks and stream terraces throughout the region are marked by an almost endless display of occupational refuse. In fact, some occupation sites are "zones" more than a mile long; others go on for longer distances and it is hard to ascertain where one site "ends" and another "begins."

What is the reason for such a great abundance of sites? Was there a huge prehistoric population? Probably not. Actually, this pattern reflects the activities of rather small population units who were frequently on the move, pursuing their hunting and gathering existence. The occupation sites represent camping and resource exploitation areas that were used recurrently over many hundreds, if not thousands, of years. This situation is described in more detail in Chapter 6.

Let us look at two kinds of occupation sites found in south Texas: one a surface-exposed site, the other, a site buried in stream silts.

Erosion, often helped along by cultivation, cattle grazing, ranch roads, and droughts, has exposed many prehistoric occupation sites. In some cases, particularly in Starr County, erosion has been so severe that sites have been completely exposed, the artifacts of thousands of years mixed together, and then covered over again by more recent silting and deposition. Such sites are likely to be of little value archaeologically. In some other areas, notably in Dimmit and Webb Counties, sheet erosion on hill slopes has exposed vast occupation sites. The array of artifacts one finds on these sites represents a mixture of time periods, as all of the specimens have been let down on a common surface by the erosion of the deposits in which they were buried (Fig. 4.1).

Surface-exposed sites are "fragile." When collection is made, the evidence is gone and cannot be replaced. Thus, even casual collecting distorts our picture of what the site was like. As pointed out in Chapter 1, such sites should be collected by controlled methods. Sites of this sort, despite erosion, can still tell us a lot.

Even a casual, uncontrolled collection from a *specific* surface-exposed site can contribute to the prehistoric record. However, it is critical that the materials from such sites be kept separate and apart from those of other sites for such collections to have maximum archaeological value.

Mr. and Mrs. L. D. White provided me with the opportunity, in the late 1960's, to study their collection from the Ouline site, La Salle County (41 LS 3). This site had been exposed by gullying, sheet erosion, and cultivation over an area of about forty acres. Numerous flint flakes, occasional artifacts, and scattered fire-cracked rock littered the surface. Mr. and Mrs. White had collected from the site for a number of years and had kept the collection intact. At the time of the study, no extensive archaeological reports existed for LaSalle County, and the Ouline materials provided a chance to identify major artifact categories in the area.

The collection consisted of 412 specimens. These included 145 dart points which were classified into 17 existing types, ranging in age from Late Paleo-Indian (Angostura) to Late Archaic (Ensor, Frio, and others). Most were typical south Texas triangular or unstemmed forms, such as Matamoros, Tortugas, Desmuke, and Catan. However, types more common in central Texas (such as Pedernales) and in southwest Texas (such as Langtry) were also present.

Only 15 arrow points came from the site, primarily the Perdiz and Scallorn types so common in south Texas (see later in this chapter). There were also more than 50 crude bifacial tools, which we called "knives" at the time; most are probably preforms, or unfin-

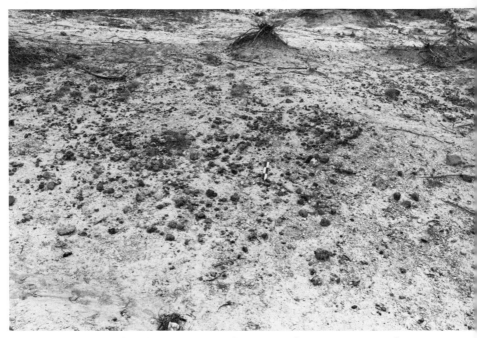

Figure 4.1. **An Eroded Surface Site in South Texas**. In this view in Live Oak County, erosion has removed upper soil deposits, exposing hearthstones, stone tools, snails, and other cultural debris. (The north arrow near the center of the photograph is 30 cm long.)

ished dart points. There were nearly 90 scrapers at Oulline, and because of the large sample, we were able to suggest a new scraper type for south Texas, called Nueces (see Fig. 5.12). Cores, choppers, drills, "gouges", and other lithics were described in our report, as well as a single mano or grinding stone.

There are problems, of course, with such a collection. The materials were mixed together on a common surface, and the range of projectile point types covered the past 8,000 years. However, the sizable sample enabled tabulations which suggested those types that were important for the area. It also permitted comparisons with central and southwest Texas sites, and with materials reported from northeastern Mexico, and it allowed a series of questions to be examined in future studies (Hester, White, and White 1969: 158-164).

Large collections of this sort from eroded sites in south Texas are still important. We are a long way from the final definition of artifact types and their distribution.

Buried occupation sites have received attention from archaeologists mainly in the last decade. These sites are found along stream
channels and their terraces where flood-deposited silts have covered ancient camping sites. In some cases, there is little on the
surface to hint at the presence of a deep, buried archaeological
deposit. Checking gopher and badger hole backdirt, gullies, eroded
bluffs, and the like can provide clues. Or the site surface may be
littered with materials, and testing is required to ascertain whether
or not buried deposits still remain intact.

In our experience, the excavation of buried occupation sites is
difficult, as large areas have to be excavated in order to recover
enough artifacts and features (such as hearths or shell accumulations) to enable us to say something useful about the way people
lived at the site. Because of the widely scattered nature of the buried
remains, it is also hard to isolate a sequence of buried deposits and
reconstruct the local culture history. We have found *open area* or
block excavations to be the only way to obtain useful data from most
south Texas sites. (See Fig. 1.2 for a view of an open-area excavation.)

One of the first sites to be extensively excavated in south Texas
was the Mariposa site (41 ZV 83) on the Chaparrosa Ranch in Zavala
County. Excavations were conducted by the author and the 1974
archaeological field course from The University of Texas at San
Antonio. A full report was later published by John Montgomery
(1978).

The site is on the east bank of Turkey Creek, paralleling the main
channel. Our best estimates indicate that the site encompasses
about 6,000 square meters. I had originally tested the site, with a
one-meter square and a one-by-two-meter trench in 1970. In 1974,
we excavated nine two-meter square units in the central part of
the site. Since the 1970 excavations had indicated that the site was
not stratified—the deposits were more or less the same from surface
to a depth of over one meter—we used five-centimeter levels to
excavate each unit. We wanted to open up a sizable area, to take
down the deposits very slowly (hence, the five-centimeter levels),
and to plot all artifacts and debris in place, in the hope of getting
data on the patterning of aboriginal activities within the excavated
area.

The site was dug for the most part with trowel and brush, and all
materials were screened. (A view of the excavations in progress is
seen in Fig. 4.2.) Most of the artifacts and hearths were found in the

Figure 4.2. **Excavations in Progress at Site 41 ZV 83**. View of the 1974 excava-tions. Two-meter squares are being excavated in 5 cm levels; screening is being done at the left.

upper fifteen to twenty cm and represented a Late Prehistoric occu-pation (arrow points were of the Perdiz, Scallorn, and Zavala types); a deeper, Archaic occupation was noted at about forty cm, and in an eroded gully away from the excavation area. Radiocarbon dates indicated that the Late Prehistoric occupations were around A.D. 1400-1600; an earlier occupation (Archaic) was dated at A.D. 500-600.

Numerous other sites have been excavated in south Texas since then. At some only a few test pits have been dug; others have been the focus of open-area digs. In Fig. 4.3, I have illustrated a deep excavation unit at site 41 LK 31-32, studied by the Center for Archae-ological Research in the Choke Canyon Reservoir area in 1977-78. This very deeply buried site yielded comparatively few artifacts; however, it dates entirely from the Archaic period and has provided us with much new information on the nature and age of sites during that period. An upper occupation at the site, with large basin-shaped hearths, dates at 2400 B.C.; other radiocarbon dates from hearths and from an accumulation of mussel shells and fish bones (a trash heap representing food refuse) indicates an earlier occupation at 3300 B.C.

Figure 4.3 **Excavation of Deeply Buried Occupations at Site 41 LK 31-32, Live Oak County.** One occupation level about halfway down the unit, and represented by the hearth exposed and pedestaled on the back wall, dates to 2400 B.C. The earliest occupation at the bottom (note the shell accumulation) dates from 3300 B.C.

Occupation sites in the coastal zone are often quite different. During the Archaic, the coastal peoples north of Corpus Christi left behind *shell middens*, moundlike accumulations of shells (mainly oyster) discarded as food refuse. Occupational debris is mixed among the tightly-packed shell. Examples of shell midden sites include Kent-Crane and Johnson (Campbell 1947, 1952), both in Aransas County.

Also during the Archaic and the Late Prehistoric periods, coastal peoples between Corpus Christi and Brownsville chose *clay dunes* as spots for occupation. These are knolls along creeks and bays created by the windblown accumulation and subsequent compaction of clay pellets. The winds blowing over the dunes scour out depressions behind them, and these fill with fresh water after rains. The clay dune affords an elevated camping area, exposed to the prevailing southeast winds; it is located on a creek or bayshore providing access to aquatic resources. Furthermore, there is often fresh water behind the dune and the view from the dune overlooks the prairie hunting areas nearby.

Clay dune sites are well known from Oso Creek, Nueces County, the Baffin and Grullo Bays of Kleberg and Kenedy Counties, and along the coast of the Rio Grande Delta (Mallouf, Baskin, and Killen 1977). They are often severely eroded, exposing thousands of land snails, baked clay lumps (at times used as hearthstones in this stoneless area), marine shells, and bits of pottery and flint. Burials were sometimes placed in the dunes (Hester 1969a).

No dune site has ever been thoroughly excavated although J. E. Corbin, the author, Al Wesolowsky, and others extensively tested the Kirchmeyer site, 41 NU 11, on Oso Creek in Nueces County in 1969. The dune deposits are extremely hard and cultural remains are widely scattered. Old buried dune surfaces appear as dark, organic-stained zones.

Finally, we should note the *burned rock midden* sites that occur along the edge of the Edwards Plateau (Fig. 4.4). The middens are of varying forms or types and these have never been adequately classified. Some of the moundlike middens have much occupational debris indicating that prehistoric peoples camped on and around them. The soil is dark and ash-stained, and fist-sized, fire-cracked rocks are everywhere. Another type of burned rock midden, often somewhat dome-shaped, is comprised of little else than burned rock with a small amount of ashy soil. Few or no artifacts occur in these. This type of burned rock midden may represent a specialized food-cooking or plant-processing area, or they may be "dumps" of burned rock cleared out of the hearths in the surrounding occupation area (Hester 1970, 1971a). There is a lot of controversy over the nature and function of various kinds of burned rock middens; much more work by professionals and amateurs is required to help unravel these.

WORKSHOP SITES

These sites represent specific activities of the ancient hunters and gatherers—mostly the procuring of chert (flint) and other chippable stone and producing from it the various flaked stone artifacts used by these societies. They are typically found on high stream terraces overlooking rivers and creeks. These terraces are capped with cobbles, often of the Uvalde gravels (and along the Rio Grande, the Rio Grande Gravels). The ancient flintworker went to these places to select suitable stone for artifact manufacture. Areas in which good chert cobbles were found became quarries and workshops, and much debris remains on the surface.

Since these were places for the initial phases of artifact-making, few complete points or other tools are found. Typical of the debris are "tested" cobbles (where the flintknapper had knocked off a piece of the cobble to see if it was good material), cortex-covered flakes representing the removal of the exterior of the cobbles in order to get set up for the production of choice interior flakes, cores that have been exhausted through flake removal, cores broken during that process, and artifacts that were started but then were broken by a poor knapping blow or by a flaw in the material.

TEMPORARY OR AUXILIARY SITES

The workshops just described are "temporary" in the sense that they were used sporadically; they were, however, repeatedly returned to by the aboriginal flintknapper. On the other hand, there are a multitude of sites in south Texas that had brief, one-time utilization either in hunting or food-gathering activities. Such sites were auxiliary to the occupation site, with the hunting or gathering party traveling out from the living area in search of food. A hunting party away from camp overnight would construct a simple hearth, repair their hunting equipment (leading to the discard of broken points, or the resharpening of point tips or knives which left flakes scattered about), and prepare a meal or two. Such limited and short-term activities would leave very little archaeological evidence.

Another temporary site might be created when certain plant foods were collected and processed before being taken back to camp. An agave might be processed by cutting off the leaves and digging up the root or bulb. What we know of agave-processing suggests that this task would leave little or no archaeological record.

Figure 4.4. **A Burned Rock Midden in South Central Texas**. The knoll-like prominence in the center (with an oak tree growing out of the middle of it) is a burned rock midden in Real County. Note the man at the left for scale.

(See the study of agave-processing by Mexican nationals witnessed by T. C. Hill, Jr., in Zavala County, in Hill, Holdsworth, and Hester 1972.)

Some temporary or auxiliary sites could be returned to from time to time for *special activities* such as harvesting a type of plant that grew seasonally in a certain locale. We get clues to this sort of thing, but rarely a clear picture of the function of the site. Site 41 ZV 109, a gravel hilltop on the Chaparrosa Ranch, had an eroded surface littered with Clear Fork tools (see Chapter 5). Wear-pattern studies of such tools have indicated that they might have been used in woodworking (Hester, Gilbow, and Albee 1973). Was this a locale of a workshop for this kind of task, or were these adze- or gouge-like tools also used to process plant materials, as in the shredding of agave leaves to obtain fibers?

Hill and Hester (1971) report a site in Zavala County (41 ZV 34) that had two separate and distinct areas which seem to reflect temporary or special activity of different time periods. In one area, there was a hearth with flakes scattered around it for a distance of twenty or thirty feet. Several artifacts were also present; these included two Archaic period dart points, a chopping tool, two crude scrapers, a notched flake of the sort used in wood-shaving, some cores and grindstone fragments. The variety, yet small number, of artifacts associated with the cooking area or hearth suggest that perhaps this was a temporary occupation for a small group of hunters and gatherers on the move through the area.

Nearby, another scatter of artifacts was recorded. These included Late Prehistoric arrow points and twenty-five to thirty small flakes. Some burned clay lumps, perhaps resulting from a small fire built on the clayey surface, were also noted. This little cluster of materials is what we might expect to remain from the encampment of a hunting party for a very brief period—perhaps overnight.

KILL-SITES

A kill-site is a spot where ancient hunters have killed and butchered an animal—or perhaps a herd of animals. Best known are the mammoth kill-sites of Clovis times and the bison kills of the Folsom and Late Paleo-Indian periods. Sites of major kills, especially of this antiquity, are not known in south Texas. However, at Bonfire Shelter in Val Verde County bison-kill episodes of Folsom and Plainview times have been documented. Small herds of bison were driven over a canyon rim, falling to their death (or at least serious injury!) below. The hunters then butchered the animals; left behind were masses of bison bones and several distinctive points that had been embedded in the animal carcasses (Fig. 4.5; Dibble and Lorrain 1967).

In south Texas, the only kill-site yet recorded is Skillet Mountain #4, 41 MC 222, along the Frio River drainage in McMullen County. It was found during UTSA archaeological investigations in the Choke Canyon Reservoir basin. The remains of several bison lay just beneath the surface. They had been butchered and various tools were mixed in and around the bones (Fig. 4.6). This kill-site dates to Late Prehistoric times, as evidenced by the presence of arrow points and radiocarbon dates of A.D. 1260-1290.

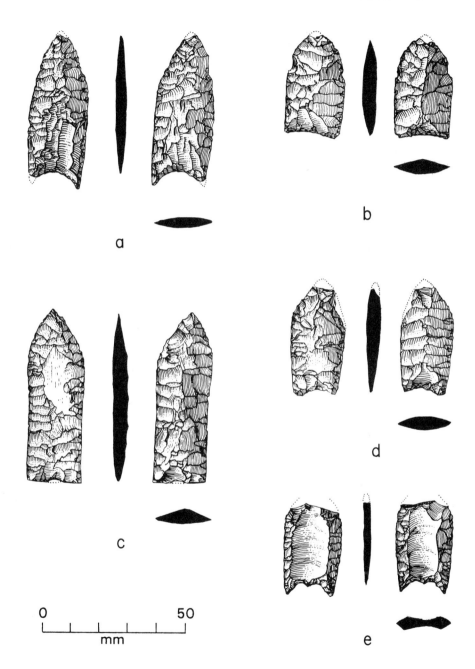

Figure 4.5. **Artifacts from the Bonfire Shelter Bison-Kill Site**. a-d, Plainview points; e, Folsom point. (From Dibble and Lorrain 1967: Fig. 14 courtesy of the Texas Memorial Museum; drawings by Hal Story.)

Figure 4.6. **Skillet Mountain Site: Kill and Butchering Locality.** Shown here is part of the excavated bison-butchering area at site 41 MC 222 in McMullen County. Note the concentration of bones in the upper right. (Photograph courtesy UTSA Center for Archaeological Research, Nueces River Project.)

ISOLATED FINDS AND CACHES

Occasionally, artifacts representing some specific activity or episode are found either away from a site or specially placed within the boundaries of a site. As to the former, the most common is the isolated find. This is most often a projectile point lying on the surface without any other evidence of cultural activity anywhere to be seen. Such finds are probably hunting losses, the result of a spear or arrow that missed its target and was not recovered by the hunter. The shaft rotted away, leaving the stone point as the only testimony to the hunt.

Caches (special clusters of artifacts) are sometimes found within or near sites. Such groups of artifacts can represent several functions, utilitarian or ceremonial, and are open to a wide range of interpretations. A metate found turned over and with a mano beneath it may represent a set of food-processing tools too unwieldy to carry along to the next occupation site; they may have been hidden away for use on the next visit to the site. A group of large bifaces or a cluster of cores and flakes may represent a flint-working inventory hidden or stored for some reason and then forgotten. Or they might be trade items which were cached away but never retrieved. The discovery and reporting of caches is important because they help to give us a bit more information on the behavior of the ancient populations.

ISOLATED BURIALS

The south Texas hunters and gatherers seem to have disposed of their dead most often as single interments in or near their occupation areas. Typically, the burials are flexed (almost in a fetal position) with few or no grave goods accompanying the skeleton.

An example of an isolated burial found within a prehistoric occupation site is reported by Hester and others (1975) from site 41 ZV 152 along Palo Blanco Creek in northern Zavala County. A bulldozer trench had cut through the site area and had exposed a burial approximately one foot below the ground surface. Excavation of the burial by T. C. Hill, Jr., led to the recovery of the skeletal remains of a female, perhaps 55-60 years of age at the time of death. Examination of the bones by a physical anthropologist revealed evidence of an arthritic condition, as well as indications from tooth enamel of a metabolic upset, an illness, or perhaps malnutrition. Associated with the burial were several small tubular bone beads, made from segments of bird or small mammal bone (Fig. 4.7). Although the burial was near the surface, it was within ancient deposits with artifacts that dated it to Archaic or perhaps Late Prehistoric times.

A few of the isolated burials are extended—the skeleton lying on its back and stretched full-length. An example of this type of burial comes from site 41 DM 40 on the Buckhorn Ranch, Dimmit County. A gully cutting across this extensive prehistoric site exposed some human bones, and excavations by J. W. House, the author, and student amateur archaeologists were able to expose and record the skeleton (Fig. 4.8). No grave goods were found and it was not possible to determine the prehistoric period during which the burial was made.

There are numerous other instances, both published and unpublished, of the discovery and excavation of isolated burials in the south Texas area. It is important that these finds be treated very carefully, excavated with skill, and promptly reported to professional archaeologists. It is from burials that we will gradually learn more about the physical stature, average life span, and medical infirmities of the prehistoric populations of the region.

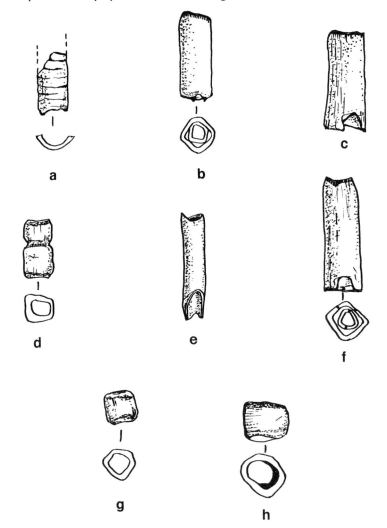

Figure 4.7. **Bone Beads from Burial at Site 41 ZV 152, Zavala County.** Lengths of specimens range from 6 mm to 26 mm. End views are shown for several specimens; note that specimens b and f have smaller beads telescoped inside.

Right, Figure 4.8. **Isolated Burial at the Buckhorn Site (41 DM 40), Dimmit County.** Note paintbrushes at left for scale; north is to the right. The burial has been pedestaled to facilitate the removal of the skeletal parts.

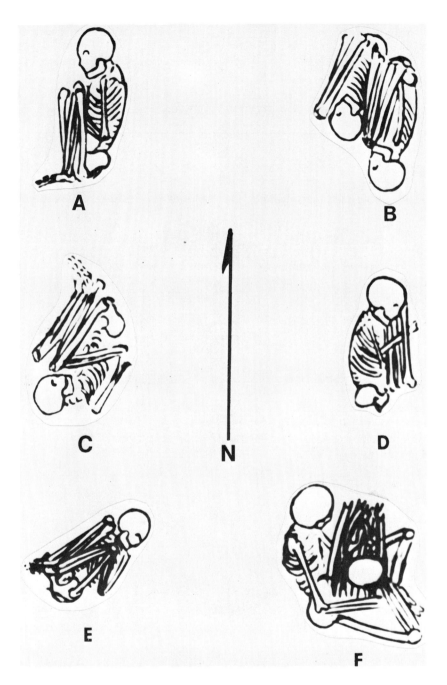

Figure 4.9. **Examples of Burial Positions at the Floyd Morris Cemetery Site in Cameron County.** (From Collins, Hester, and Weir 1969.)

CEMETERIES

Several cemetery sites, with burials of up to a hundred or more individuals, have been documented along the south Texas coast. Some of these are in the Rio Grande Delta region and date to the Late Prehistoric Brownsville Complex. Sites like Floyd Morris (41 CF 2; Cameron County) and Ayala (41 HG 1; Hidalgo County) contained fifteen to eighteen burials, all in flexed positions and some with associated grave goods (Fig. 4.9).

The grave goods were generally ornaments made of shell (Fig. 4.10), although at the Floyd Morris site they also included projectile points, scrapers, beads made of human bone, and two stone beads, one of which was made of jadeite (a stone that would have to have been imported in ancient times from Mexico).*

One of the most interesting burials at the Floyd Morris site was Burial 11 (Fig. 4.11). The skeleton of a young female (15-16 years of age) rested on the back with the shoulders and upper back slightly elevated; the legs were loosely flexed and spread apart. The arms were placed along the sides of the body and were slightly flexed at the elbows, with the hands resting between the thighs and above the pelvis. Resting on the abdominal region of this female were the closely clustered but disarticulated bones of an adult male (probably 40 years old). Not all of the bones of the male were present. Those that did occur in this "bundle burial" (as such disarticulated clusters are called) were coated with a dark substance (unidentified) and painted with a red pigment (probably made from hematite); some of the long bones had been cut at the ends and "plugged" with pieces of asphaltum. Beneath this male bundle burial and within the pelvis area of the female burial were the remains of either a newborn infant or a fetus. It could not be determined if these tiny skeletal remains were intra-uterine or laid on the abdomen of the female at the time of burial.

About 300 beads, mostly made of sections of human bone, were found with this burial group. Some shell beads and bone beads were scattered among the bones in the adult male bundle burial.

How can we interpret these burials—a young female, with the bones of an adult male resting on her lap and those of a newborn infant, possibly a fetus, also present? While we do not yet have any

*Papers by Collins, Hester, and Weir (1969), Hester (1969b), and Hester and Rodgers (1971) provide details on these sites.

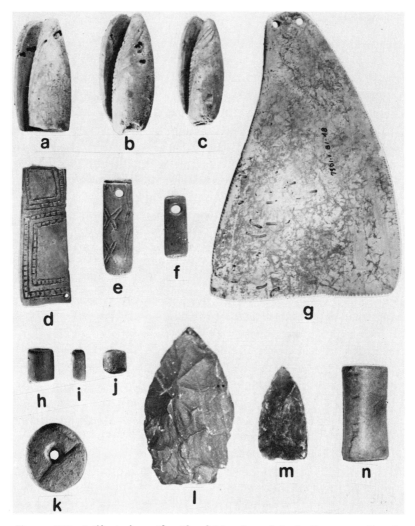

Figure 4.10. **Artifacts from the Floyd Morris and Ayala Cemetery Sites in Cameron and Hidalgo Counties.** a-c, olive shell tinkler and beads; d-f, carved bone pendants; g, shell pendant; h-j, tubular bone beads; k, stone bead; l-m, stone bifaces; n, jadeite bead. Length of g is 16.4 cm.

direct evidence to link the peoples of the Brownsville Complex to the historic Coahuilteco peoples of the lower Rio Grande Valley, an interesting situation was recorded by the Spanish among the peoples known as the Carrizo, who lived in Cameron County in early historic times. It was reported that if a woman died during

Figure 4.11. **Burial 11 from the Floyd Morris Cemetery Site in Cameron County.**

childbirth, the woman's body was buried along with that of the child, even if the newborn was alive and well. This seems gruesome by our standards, but in a hunting and gathering population it may have been done by necessity if no one else in the group could care for the infant. Or is this the burial of a young female who died before childbirth?

What about the bones, painted and cut, of the adult male? Only the top part of the skull was there with the other bones, and it looked as if the skull had been modified. Had it been used as a skull drinking cup of the type the Spaniards had seen in other Coahuilteco groups? Probably not. Were these the bones of the female's husband, or father, or some other relative who died or was killed some distance from home, then buried and later exhumed and the bones brought back to his group? Such "ancestor reverence" and the curation of the bones of deceased relatives is found around the world in many primitive populations. In the light of the treatment accorded to these bones, it looks as if they had some special significance. What that was we will probably never know.

Other cemetery sites occur up the coast between Baffin Bay and Corpus Christi Bay. Small prehistoric cemeteries have been found along Grullo Bay east of Kingsville. Here too, artifacts made from human long bones were found with some burials (Hester 1969c). Most are bone tubes or beads (Fig. 4.12) occasionally coated with reddish pigment, again probably hematite.

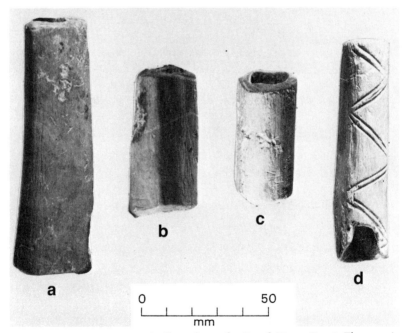

Figure 4.12. **Human Bone Artifacts from the South Texas Coast**. The specimens shown here are from cemetery sites in Kleberg County. Note incised lines on specimen d.

Along Oso Bay and Oso Creek south of Corpus Christi occur the greatest known concentration of cemetery sites in the region. These cemeteries, like those in the Brownsville region, are usually placed on the edge or away from the occupation sites. On the Oso, the most prominent topographic features are the clay dunes, and these were used either for occupations or for cemeteries. No report has ever been published on the largest cemetery on Oso Bay. It is 41 NU 2 (Fig. 4.13), initially excavated by The University of Texas in the 1930s. There had been some earlier digging at the site but it was uncontrolled. We know that between the uncontrolled probes and the large-scale university excavations, the skeletons of well over 100 individuals were found. That the cemetery had been repeatedly used for many years was evidenced by the fact that older burials had been disturbed by more recent ones, and scattered bones of the prior interments were often mixed with the articulated skeleton of the latter. The burials were flexed and very few grave goods were found. In the typical burial pattern, the skeleton is flexed on its side with the head directed toward the creek; the legs are tightly folded and extending perpendicular from the pelvis. The arms are pulled up in front of the chest and the hands opened over the face (Fig. 4.14).

Up Oso Creek other cemeteries have been found, but most have not been properly dug and most of their scientific value has been lost. At one site, 41 NU 29, one of the burials had a stemmed Archaic dart point embedded in the vertebra; this is one of the few instances where the direct cause of death can be ascertained in the hundreds of burials excavated along the creek and bay. Grave goods in the creek-side cemetery sites are also rare. One spectacular find was that of three large triangular bone artifacts, apparently made from bison scapulas. These had been shaped and polished and were decorated with incised lines and drilled pits (see Fig. 4.15). They were associated with the burial of a young adult male.

It is unfortunate that over the years, the news media have usually reported these cemeteries as "burial grounds of Karankawa cannibals." Some books have also included such sensational descriptions. While we usually cannot date these cemeteries with great precision, most of them appear to date from Archaic times and can in no way be linked to the historic Karankawa.

Some other prehistoric cemeteries are known from the Corpus Christi area, including the Odem burial site found in the early 1950s

Figure 4.13. **The Oso Cemetery Site (41 NU 2), Nueces County.** (Photograph courtesy of the Texas Archeological Research Laboratory, The University of Texas at Austin.)

Figure 4.14. **Burial at the Oso Cemetery Site (41 NU 2).**
Skull at back of the burial is from an earlier, disturbed
interment.

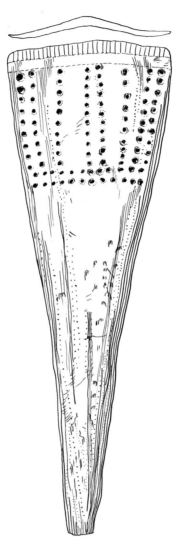

Figure 4.15. **Bison Scapula Artifact from Burial at 41 NU 29, Nueces County.** Length of specimen is 27 cm. Cross section is shown at top.

and two burial sites near Ingleside, reported by Hester and Corbin (1975). At one of these sites, 41 SP 78 (San Patricio County), large cockle shells were in one of the graves, apparently having served as scoops in digging the grave. Similar finds have been reported from Oso Creek.

Amateur archaeologists are often called upon to salvage information from prehistoric cemeteries that have been exposed by development. In 1978-79, Edward R. Mokry, Jr., almost singlehandedly documented a small cemetery uncovered by bulldozers at the location of a housing subdivision in Corpus Christi. This site (41 NU 173) is a very important one and yielded evidence of more than thirteen burials (Fig. 4.16). Among the few grave artifacts was a Scallorn arrow point, apparently in the chest area of Burial 4B. This helps us to date the cemetery to Late Prehistoric times. The site was, however, subjected to vandalism and uncontrolled digging by looters. Since it is on private property, the site could not be protected by the State's antiquities laws. Though the landowner and developer were cooperative, the site is, at this writing, essentially destroyed. Were it not for Mokry's careful work, we would know nothing about this burial site.

Figure 4.16. **Burials at Site 41 NU 173, Nueces County.** Field sketch, courtesy of E. R. Mokry, Jr., of Burials 10 and 11 at the site. Burial 9, a disturbed interment, is seen at the lower left.

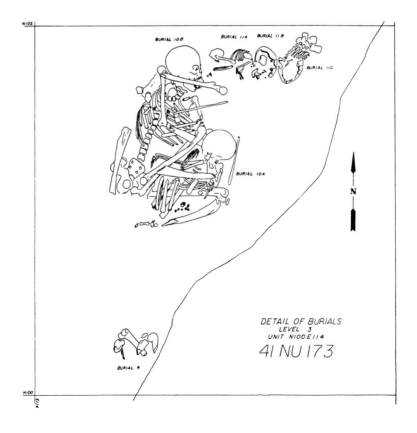

Cemeteries have been very rarely found in the interior of south Texas; isolated burials seem to have been the usual pattern there. However, in 1977 the construction of Interstate Highway 37 near Three Rivers led to the discovery of site 41 LK 28. Archaeologists from the Texas Department of Highways and Public Transportation began excavations at this site, which they named Loma Sandia. After a period of initial testing and excavation, several burials were exposed. The area around the burials was expanded and more skeletons were found. Over a period of several months, more than 180 burials were discovered.

This impressive cemetery (Fig. 4.17) is highly significant in south Texas prehistoric studies. Many of the burials had associated grave offerings. Some seemed to be ceremonial such as the horns of whitetail deer placed over a burial. (Sometimes these racks had been burned, probably part of a burial ritual.) Other burials had large, tubular stone pipes and ornaments of conch shell placed with them. Dart points of Archaic age were found with other burials, as well as chunks of flint, flakes, and other materials relating to stoneworking. Some of these may have been the personal property of the dead individual, or perhaps they were placed in the grave for use in the afterlife. Charles Johnson II, the supervisory archaeologist, is preparing a report on this site.

ROCK ART SITES

Rock art in primitive cultures generally takes two forms: petroglyphs (designs carved or engraved on stone surfaces) and pictographs (motifs painted on such surfaces). Pictograph sites are very well documented in the area about the mouth of the Pecos in southwest Texas. The dry, protected shelters or caves in the steep-walled canyons of the Rio Grande, Devil's, and Pecos Rivers (and their many tributaries) contain a rich pictographic art, dating back thousands of years.

Much of this art is, to modern eyes, "abstract"—various geometric and linear designs. Other motifs are naturalistic, depicting deer, panthers, and humans. This art is polychrome, principally red,

Right, Figure 4.17. **The Loma Sandia Site (41 LK 28), Live Oak County**. Aerial view of this Archaic period cemetery site, excavated by Texas Department of Highways and Public Transportation archaeologists. (Photograph courtesy of Charles Johnson II.)

yellow, black, and blue. Rock art of later times, during the Late Prehistoric, is usually executed only in reds and shows scenes of men
armed with bows and arrows pursuing deer or deer herds. Both the
Archaic polychrome art and the Late Prehistoric art probably represent activities of hunting cults. There is a beautifully illustrated book
on the rock art of this area—as well as other parts of Texas—*The Rock
Art of Texas Indians* by Forrest Kirkland and W. W. Newcomb, Jr.
(University of Texas Press, Austin).

In south Texas, only one rock art site is known. At 41 WB 56 on
the Rio Grande in Webb County there is a polychrome panel on
the back wall of a sandstone overhang. The panel is over four meters
(thirteen feet) long and consists largely of broad zigzag designs
(see Fig. 4.18); colors are mostly red and yellow. A report on the site
is under preparation by the author.

Parts of northeastern Mexico have a rich rock art, particularly
in the slopes and foothills of the Sierra Madre Oriental in Nuevo
Leon. Petroglyphs are the most common, with geometric, linear,
and dot designs. Recent studies have been conducted by William
Breen Murray of the University of Monterrey.

Below, Figure 4.18. **Rock Art Panel at Site 41 WB 56.** The polychrome art
panel is protected by a sandstone overhang. The site overlooks the Rio
Grande. Length of panel, from left to right, about 4 meters.

Right, Figure 4.19. **Baker Cave (41 VV 213), Val Verde County.** View of 1976
excavations. Area of 9,000-year-old occupations is at the back of the cave.

ROCKSHELTER AND CAVE SITES

These sites are not found in south Texas, principally because the topography is inappropriate. However, some sandstone overhangs (of the type at 41 WB 56 noted above) that may have served as temporary camping places are known to occur in bluffs on the middle Nueces River and on the Rio Grande. Along the edge of the Edwards Plateau, rockshelter occupations are known for the Late Archaic and Late Prehistoric periods. Some were used for even longer time spans. For example, Scorpion Cave on the upper Medina River, had intensive and long-term occupations (Highly et al. 1978). Other shelters have been found in northern Uvalde County.

The best known rockshelter sites are from the lower Devil's and Pecos River drainages and in the canyons of the Rio Grande in Val Verde County. These contain dry, dusty deposits which are often quite deep and can contain well-preserved artifacts of wood and plant fiber (sandals, baskets, etc.). While a number of rockshelter sites have been excavated by professional and amateur archaeologists, many more have been looted and destroyed by relic-collectors digging for artifacts. This kind of digging not only destroys irreplaceable scientific evidence . . . it can be hazardous to your health. Unless a proper mask is worn, the fine dust particles in these dry caves can settle in the lungs and eventually cause problems of the sort experienced by coal miners.

An example of a site carefully excavated and subsequently published by amateur archaeologists is Baker Cave (Fig. 4.19). James Word led these excavations in the 1960s (Word and Douglas 1970). Baker Cave has dry deposits more than eleven feet deep and with a sequence of 9,000 years of human occupation. Word's work was followed up by a team led by the author in 1976 (Hester 1979). Between them, they have produced data on cultural and climatic change beginning with the Golondrina Complex of 7000 B.C. and going up to the Late Prehistoric period, after A.D. 1000. Although some uncontrolled digging has gone on in the cave, the landowner appreciates the importance of the cave deposits to archaeology and has protected the site from looters.

5
MAJOR ARTIFACT TYPES OF SOUTH TEXAS

We know, both from Spanish accounts and from excavations in the dry caves of the southwest Texas area, that the region's native populations had an extensive array of artifacts fashioned from wood, leather, hide, and plant fibers. Rockshelters in Val Verde County, southwest Texas, have yielded well-preserved sandals, baskets, woven rabbit-fur robes, cordage and string of various sizes, and many other items of clothing and personal possessions.

However, in south Texas none of these has survived. Only the hardiest artifacts are left: those made of chipped stone, ground stone, bone, shell, and antler. The relatively humid climate, acting on the usually unsheltered occupation sites of this region, has destroyed the more perishable items. Occasionally an object will be recovered with some vestige of decoration, such as a painted pebble (Fig. 5.1) found eroding from a site on the Nueces River near La Pryor (Hester 1977a). Such finds shed little light on what must have been an extensive material culture in prehistoric times. We have to attempt a reconstruction of the ancient lifeways with only a partial record of their implements and weapons.

Before reviewing the major types or classes of artifacts found in south Texas sites, it will be helpful to take a look at the processes of chipped artifact production.

MAKING STONE TOOLS

There are basically two kinds of chipped stone artifacts: bifaces and unifaces. Bifaces are those flaked on both sides, and are typified by projectile points and knives. Unifaces are flaked on one side or

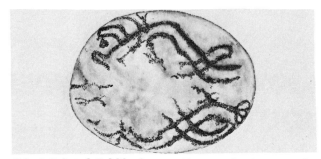

Figure 5.1. **A Painted Pebble from a Site on the Nueces River, Zavala County.** The specimen is painted with red lines. Length of the artifact is 7.8 cm.

face, usually along the edges. Scrapers are most common among artifacts in the uniface category.

A wide range of siliceous stone (usually called flint but more properly known as chert) occurs across much of southern Texas and was used in tool-making. It is conspicuously absent from the coastal zone, and the ancient peoples of that area had to obtain stone raw materials from inland. On the southwestern edge of the Edwards Plateau, the chert occurs in nodular or ledge form, eroding from limestone formations. Throughout much of the interior of southern Texas, chert and other chippable stone (quartzite, chalcedony, petrified wood, etc.) occurs in deposits of the Uvalde Gravels, which cap many hills and high stream terraces. Along the Rio Grande drainage, the often colorful siliceous Rio Grande Gravels were utilized for tool-making.

In most cases, the making of an artifact involves a specific set of activities—a process which leaves a lot of waste, such as the flakes and cores from which they were struck. And in the course of artifact manufacture, many artifacts are broken or discarded because of flint-knapper error or flaws in the material.

In a paper published in 1975, I outlined some of the aspects of the chipped stone manufacturing process for south Texas, based on research done at the Chaparrosa Ranch (Hester 1975; 1978). An example from this study will serve to demonstrate some of the major steps in stone tool-making. Along Chaparrosa and Turkey Creeks in northern Zavala County are deposits of Uvalde Gravels, high on stream terraces. The gravels are in cobble form; some are grainy and tough and are useless for tool-making, while others have a finer grain and were selected for knapping.

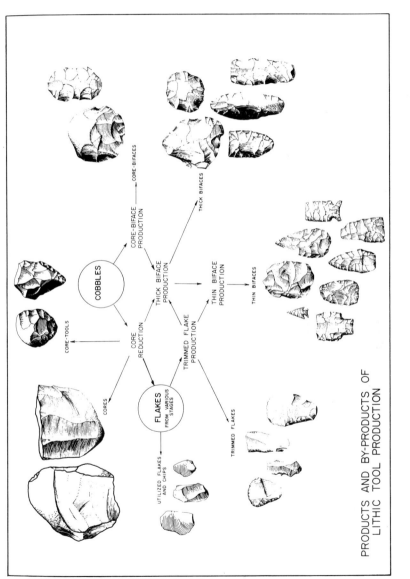

Figure 5.2 **The Tool-Making Process.** Illustrated here is the sequence of stone tool-making reconstructed from studies in the Cuero Reservoir area, Dewitt and Gonzales Counties. (Fox et al., 1974: Figure 8; courtesy of the Texas Historical Commission.)

The manufacture of a lithic tool is a reduction process. One starts with a piece of stone, shapes it into final form . . . all the while reducing it in size and mass and creating a series of telltale by-products. The chipped stone process in the Chaparrosa study area began on the high terraces, in the exposures of Uvalde Gravels. The aboriginal stoneworker would leave his stream-side campsite and go up to the gravel deposits. He would pick through the gravels, striking specimens with his hammerstone in order to remove a piece here and there, testing the quality of the rock.

Once a suitable cobble was found, the process began (Fig. 5.2). The cobble was split by a sharp blow with the hammerstone (the hammerstones are often made, in south Texas, of a hard purple-to-brown quartzite). Such a break created a flat, smooth chipping surface known as the *striking platform*. Once this platform had been established, the knapper began to shape the cobble fragment, creating a *core*. This entailed the removal of the exterior surface—the *cortex*—of the cobble. Such removals produced *flakes*, in this case called "primary cortex flakes" since they were removed in the early stage of reduction (Fig. 5.3). Further shaping of the core produced "secondary cortex flakes", with the exteriors of these flakes bearing remnants of the cobble cortex and scars from previous flake removals (Fig. 5.3).

Generally, the knapper was after "interior flakes", free of cortex and from the interior part of the core. Long, rather thick interior flakes could be produced, and the best of these were selected for the making of projectile points, knives, or other tools. Of course, some of the primary and secondary flakes were also used at times in the manufacture of tools, especially scrapers.

When the knapper had formed his core, the data from Chaparrosa indicate that he could either produce flakes at the workshop or simply shape the core and take it back to the camp.

Once a suitable flake (or probably a series of flakes to have on hand for later chipping needs) was produced, work could begin on the tool. We suspect that the knapper had a "mental template" of what he was going to make; he could look at the flake and see in it the finished shape of the point he was seeking to produce.

The initial phases of the knapping process we have described were done by *percussion* techniques (Fig. 5.4), using a hammerstone. Percussion continued to be used as the process went along. First, the flake was given rough shape by controlled percussion blows;

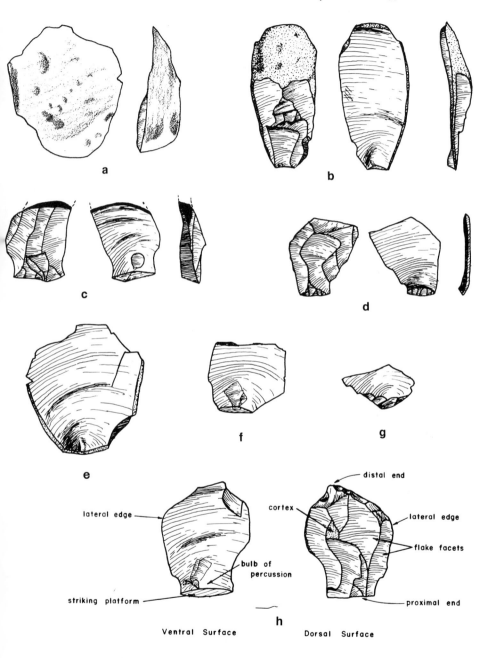

Figure 5.3. **Flake Typology.** a, primary cortex; b, secondary cortex; c, interior; d, biface thinning; e-g, various flake platform types (e, cortex; f, single facet; g, multi-facetted); h, attributes of flakes. (Drawings from Shafer 1969: Fig. 2; courtesy of Texas Archeological Survey.)

we often refer to this stage of the artifact as the "blank." Many artifact-making endeavors never got beyond this stage, as the hammerstone might strike at the wrong angle, breaking the blank, or a flaw might be discovered in the stone, leading the knapper to discard it—probably in disgust. At many south Texas sites, these blanks occur but are thought of by the collector as "crude" artifacts, the work of a "practicing" flintknapper, or as knives or choppers.

When the blank had been shaped, the knapper generally proceeded with the reduction, attempting to further shape and thin the specimen. This produced, through even more careful percussion and perhaps a switch to a smaller hammerstone or an antler percussor (Fig. 5.4), a more refined—yet still unfinished—specimen that archaeologists refer to as a *preform*. The imperfect, discarded bifaces of this stage are often called "knives" when they are found, although they had never functioned as such and simply represent a dead end in the tool-making process.

Once a preform had achieved the shape and thickness desired by the knapper, he could then proceed to give it final shape by *pressure* flaking. Most commonly used in south Texas for this purpose was a flaker made from the ulna of a deer (Fig. 5.4) or the tine end of a deer antler. With pressure flaking, the point could be given a sharp, thin edge and notches could be chipped into the sides or corners of the specimen. Or the point could be left without notches or a stem, as is common with the triangular points found throughout south Texas.

The best way to comprehend the tool-making process, and the problems encountered by the aboriginal knapper, is to try your hand at it. But be careful—the flakes come off fast and the edges are sharp! Protective goggles or glasses should be worn, and gloves are definitely advisable for the inexperienced knapper. Keep bandages at hand, and be prepared to agonize over a fingertip crunched between the hammerstone and the core! If you become seriously interested in lithic technology and experimental knapping, you might look at some of the books listed as suggested readings for this chapter.

Right, Figure 5.4. **Techniques of Stone Tool-Making**. 1, percussion, using a hammerstone; 2, pressure flaking, using a bone or antler tool; 3, "soft hammer" or billet percussion, using an antler hammer.

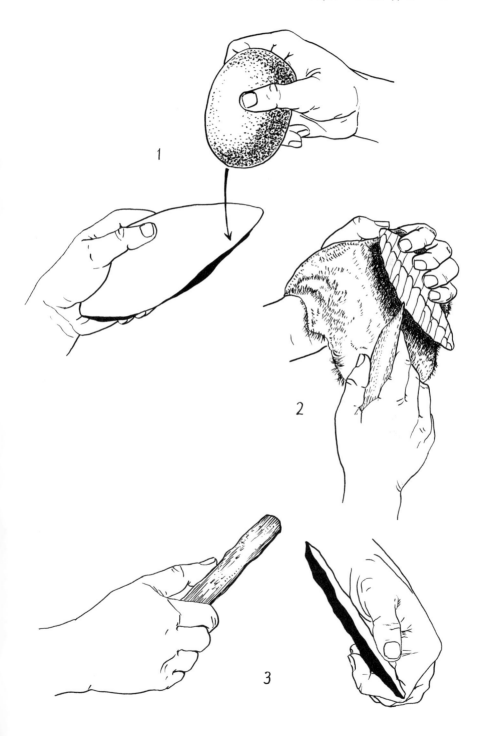

PROJECTILE POINTS

Among the most distinctive artifacts—and certainly the one that first catches the attention of the person who is becoming interested in archaeology—is the projectile point or "arrowhead."*

Projectile points are frequent on south Texas sites and are avidly sought by relic-collectors and archaeologists alike. Unfortunately, the relic-collector usually wants the specimens for their "looks", dumps them in a cigar box (or puts them in a frame on the wall), and forgets where they were found. This process destroys all scientific value of the specimens, and their removal from the place of discovery damages the potential for future research in an area. For example, when Texas A&M University carried out a major site location study in McMullen and Atascosa Counties in 1975, their archaeologists found that most sites had been stripped of projectile points. They could do very little in terms of ascertaining the ages of the sites or their cultural affiliations because of the bias introduced by relic-collecting activities.

In south Texas (and in most of the New World, for that matter), projectile points fall into two groups: *dart points* and *arrow points*. Dart points are fairly large, heavy points (the "arrowheads" of the collector), used as tips for short spears thrown with an atlatl (Fig. 5.5). They were the only weapon tips in use in south Texas for most of the prehistoric period.

*Most of the major types that are found in south Texas are briefly discussed here, and some illustrations are provided. However, amateur archaeologists wishing to learn more about such point types should see if their local library has a copy of *An Introductory Handbook of Texas Archeology* (by Dee Ann Suhm, A. D. Krieger, and E. B. Jelks; Bulletin of the Texas Archeological Society, Vol. 25, 1954) or *Handbook of Texas Archeology: Type Descriptions* (by Suhm and Jelks; Texas Memorial Museum and Texas Archeological Society, 1962). Both books are, at this writing, out of print and can be purchased only in a used-book store. However, the Anthropology Club of West Texas State University (Canyon) has printed a large wall poster which illustrates most Texas point types, including several defined since the time of Suhm and Jelk's 1962 volume. In addition, most Texas point types are described and illustrated in the several volumes of *A Guide to Certain American Indian Projectile Points*, published by the Oklahoma Anthropological Society.

Right, Figure 5.5. **Using a Spearthrower.** This artist's reconstruction shows the use of a spear and spearthrower or *atlatl*, the main weapons of the Archaic and Paleo-Indian periods in south Texas.

When the bow and arrow was developed (about A.D. 1000 or after), the dart points were no longer used; they were generally too heavy and bulky. Late Prehistoric peoples used thin, light, and very small arrow points to tip the arrow shafts. These artifacts are commonly called "bird points", although they could have been and were used to kill anything from birds to bison (including deer, rabbits, and humans).

Major Dart Point Types.

I have listed below, in alphabetical order, most of the major dart point types found in south Texas or adjacent areas. I have indicated their approximate date or cultural period; for most, we still have little firm evidence as to precise age. More details can be found in the Suhm and Jelks volume, but I have tried to update some of their information here.

It is important to realize that the classification of a point by type is sometimes "real" (the aboriginal knapper was making a specific shape or style) and sometimes "artificial" (lumped into groups by archaeologists). Many of the latter represent not projectile points but preforms, knives, or unfinished points. It is further important to realize that in most regions of North America, dart and arrow points changed in shape through time, and at different instances in time (Fig. 5.6). We are not sure of why such style changes were made; perhaps they reflect new hunting technologies in some areas. For whatever reason, many of the styles spread widely (almost like a fad in our own society), and archaeologists can use them as "time markers" once enough excavations have been done in an area so that the sequence of point style changes is known. They also help us to define prehistoric cultural boundaries. As far as we can determine, however, specific point types or styles were *not* linked to tribal groups.

Right, Figure 5.6. **Sequence of Projectile Point Types in Central and South-Central Texas**. Based on excavations at Canyon Reservoir, Comal County. (From Johnson, Suhm, and Tunnell 1962; courtesy of the Texas Memorial Museum; drawings by Hal Story.)

TYPE SITES	POINT TYPES	TIME PERIODS	STAGES
Blum Smith Kyle Blum Smith Kyle	Granbury Perdiz Cliffton Scallorn	*(TOYAH FOCUS)* *(AUSTIN FOCUS)*	Neo - American
Wunderlich Smith Williams Collins	Prov Type III Darl	TRANSITIONAL	
Oblate Wunderlich Collins	Ensor Frio Montell Marcos	LATE	Archaic
Wunderlich Crumley	Pedernales Bulverde	MIDDLE	Archaic
Wunderlich Crumley	Nolan Travis	EARLY	Archaic
			Paleo - Indian

Figure 5.7

ABASOLO   Common throughout south Texas, especially in the Rio Grande drainage. Archaic.

ANGOSTURA   A Late Paleo-Indian type, ca. 6000 B.C.

BELL   Distinctive by its size and massive barbs; Pre-Archaic.

BULVERDE   Not very common in south Texas; principally a central Texas form of the Early Archaic.

CARRIZO   Triangular with deep basal notch. Found primarily in Dimmit, Zavala, La Salle, and Frio Counties. Archaic.

CASTROVILLE   Found at a number of south Texas sites, although mainly a central Texas form; Late Archaic (700 B.C. at Bonfire Shelter in Val Verde County). Associated with some of the burials at 41 LK 28 near Three Rivers.

CATAN   Common throughout south Texas, and perhaps should be grouped with Abasolo, representing a continuum of unstemmed round-based forms. Archaic into Late Prehistoric.

CLOVIS   The earliest known point form, dated elsewhere at 9200 B.C. Paleo-Indian.

DESMUKE   Characterized by a lozenge-shaped outline; quite common in La Salle County and adjacent areas. Archaic.

EARLY CORNER NOTCHED   This is a "series", not a type, consisting of Pre-Archaic period points with corner notched stems. They are often typed as Martindale or Uvalde but it is felt that at this stage of inquiry it is better to group them into an "Early Corner Notched" series than to try to force them into types defined originally for later periods in the Archaic. These specimens are not common in south Texas, although they have been found in Zavala County, and in the counties fringing on the edge of the Edwards Plateau.

EARLY TRIANGULAR   Triangular points of the Pre-Archaic period, principally in south-central Texas. Usually thinner than Tortugas (see below), with parallel oblique flake scars along edges, often creating a serrated effect. Base thinned by long, vertical flakes.

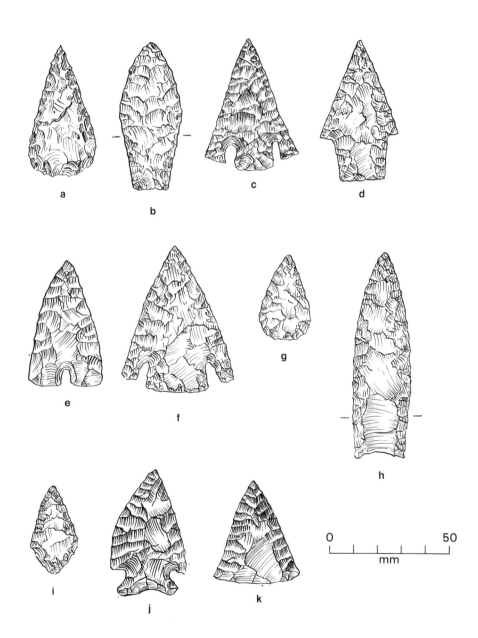

Figure 5.7. **Major Dart Point Types**. a, Abasolo; b, Angostura; c, Bell; d, Bulverde; e, Carrizo; f, Castroville; g, Catan; h, Clovis; i, Desmuke; j, Early Corner Notched; k, Early Triangular; (lines on b and h indicate extent of edge dulling).

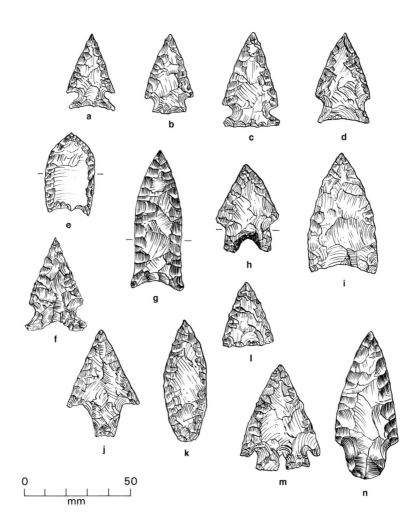

Figure 5.8. **Major Dart Point Types**. a, Edgewood; b, Ellis; c, Ensor; d, Fairland; e, Folsom; f, Frio; g, Golondrina; h, Gower; i, Kinney; j, Langtry; k, Lerma; l, Matamoros; m, Montell; n, Morhiss; (lines on e, g, h, indicate extent of edge dulling).

Figure 5.8

EDGEWOOD   This type might be applied to some of the small, stemmed Late Archaic points in south Texas.

ELLIS   Like Edgewood, it appears to be a Late Archaic (perhaps even into the Late Prehistoric) style in south Texas. In large samples, it is often hard to separate Ellis, Edgewood, Fairland, and Zavala points (see below) into distinctive groups.

ENSOR   Widespread in south Texas, in the Late Archaic and into the Late Prehistoric. It, and some of the other small dart points, could have conceivably also been used as arrow points.

FAIRLAND   Also a late Archaic style in south Texas; see comments under Ellis.

FOLSOM   Paleo-Indian point type easily recognized by its excellent chipping, thinness, and long flutes on one or both faces. Found at scattered south Texas sites. Dated around 8500-8800 B.C.

FRIO   Common in south Texas, and typical of Late Archaic times.

GOLONDRINA   Late Paleo-Indian type similar to Plainview but with flared basal corners and deep basal concavity. Radiocarbon-dated at 7000 B.C. at Baker Cave, Val Verde County.

GOWER   Pre-Archaic type found in central and south-central Texas; rarely found in south Texas. Stemmed, with an indented base; the specimens are usually rather crudely made.

KINNEY   These specimens may be knives, and some may be preforms. It is not certain if this is a "real" type. Archaic.

LANGTRY   Although this type is definitive of the Middle Archaic (ca. 1000-2000 B.C.) in adjacent southwest Texas (mouth of the Pecos area), it is frequently found in south Texas.

LERMA   Like Kinney, this may not be a "real" type. Into this category have been lumped bipointed specimens, assumed by some to be Paleo-Indian in age. In south Texas, specimens resembling Lerma are generally found in Archaic contexts.

MATAMOROS   Small, often thick, triangular points. Extremely common in south Texas. Late Archaic into Late Prehistoric (associated with ceramics) in some areas. One radiocarbon date from near Three Rivers (site 41 LK 106) places these specimens after A.D. 1250. Like Catan and Abasolo, Matamoros and the larger

Tortugas type may represent a continuum. Much research on this type is needed.

MONTELL   Not frequent in south Texas, but found at some sites in the northern part of the region. A time marker of the central Texas Late Archaic (late centuries B.C. to early centuries A.D.).

MORHISS   Found mainly on the lower reaches of the Guadalupe River in the upper part of the south Texas coastal plain. Dated to ca. 800 B.C. at site 41 GD 21 in Goliad County. There are often traces of asphaltum on the stem, resulting from the use of the gummy natural tar for hafting.

Figure 5.9

NOLAN   Not common in south Texas; typical of the Early Archaic in central Texas. Distinctive by its alternately beveled stem edges. Dated at ca. 2000 B.C. at site 41 BX 1, Bexar County, but probably extends back in time to 3000 B.C.

PALMILLAS   This is a very weak typological group including points with small rounded stems. Archaic.

PEDERNALES   Found at a number of south Texas sites, primarily in the northern sector. Typical of the Middle Archaic in central Texas (1000-2000 B.C.).

PLAINVIEW   Paleo-Indian type dated at ca. 8200 B.C. (Bonfire Shelter, Val Verde County). Predates the Golondrina form mentioned above, although the two types have some similarities. A major south-central Texas site for Plainview is 41 BX 229 (St. Mary's Hall) in San Antonio.

REFUGIO   This is not a good typological group. Most of the unstemmed, round-base specimens are either preforms or knives. Archaic?

SCOTTSBLUFF   Infrequent in south Texas. Paleo-Indian type of ca. 6500 B.C., typified by fine parallel flaking and a "fat feel" due to its biconvex cross section. A number of specimens have been reported from Victoria County.

SHUMLA   Typical of the Early Archaic (2000-3000 B.C.) of the southwest Texas area (mouth of the Pecos) but sometimes found in sites in south Texas, principally in the Rio Grande drainage. In sites in Dimmit and Zavala Counties, Shumla points are usually

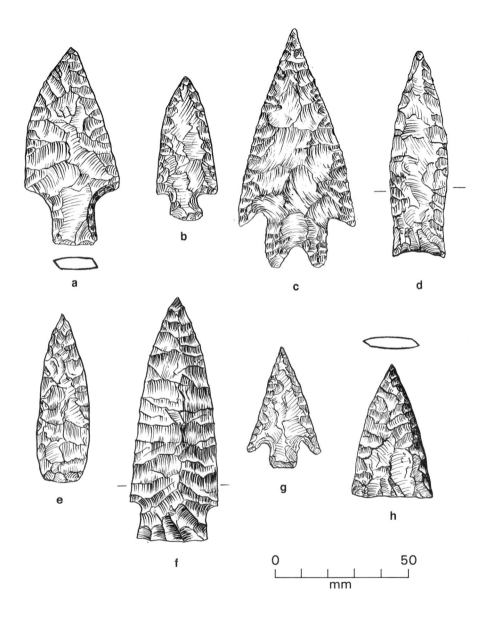

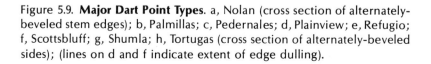

Figure 5.9. **Major Dart Point Types.** a, Nolan (cross section of alternately-beveled stem edges); b, Palmillas; c, Pedernales; d, Plainview; e, Refugio; f, Scottsbluff; g, Shumla; h, Tortugas (cross section of alternately-beveled sides); (lines on d and f indicate extent of edge dulling).

a

b

c

d

e

f

g

h

i

j

k

l

0   50
|___|___|___|___|___|
          mm

Figure 5.10. **Major Arrow Point Types**. a, "Bulbar stemmed"; b, Cameron; c, Cuney; d, Edwards; e, Fresno; f, Guerrero; g, Harrell; h, "Lozenge"; i, McGloin; j, Padre; k, Perdiz; l, Scallorn.

made of heat-treated chert. The heat treatment process (also used in other prehistoric groups scattered around the world) turns the chert to a pinkish color, and gives the surface a waxy to greasy feel.

TORTUGAS   This point type is often thought of as characteristic of south Texas archaeology. While there are typological problems, there is growing evidence that points of this form are characteristic of the Middle Archaic in south Texas, prior to 1300 B.C. (data from site ,41 LK 201, near Three Rivers). Most specimens are characterized by a triangular shape and alternately beveled edges.

Major Arrow Point Types

All of the point types described below date from the Late Prehistoric period, after A.D. 1000 in most parts of south Texas.

Figure 5.10

"BULBAR STEMMED"   These points are very similar to Perdiz (see below) and may represent a regional variant of that type in the Corpus Christi area on the coast. Corbin (1974) believes they are a separate type.

CAMERON   Tiny, triangular arrow points found in the Rio Grande Delta and along the coast up to the Baffin Bay area. Exact dating within the Late Prehistoric is not known. The type persisted into Historic times, as some specimens are made of glass.

CLIFFTON   (see Perdiz)

CUNEY   This type is typical of East Texas, but specimens are occasionally found in south Texas (as at site 41 DM 33 in Dimmit County).

EDWARDS   Found in south central Texas, principally on the southern Edwards Plateau. These points have often been confused with Scallorn (see below) in the past, but it has been demonstrated that they are a separate and earlier type. In fact, they are probably the first arrow points to appear in that area. At the La Jita site (41 UV 21; Uvalde County), the type is dated at A.D. 960-1040 (Hester 1971a). Similar dates come from sites 41 BX 36 and 41 BX 377 on Camp Bullis in northern Bexar County (Gerstle, Kelly, and Assad 1978).

FRESNO   It is hard to be sure if this is a "real" type in all cases. Many triangular specimens of this size are actually arrow point pre-forms (see Highley et al. 1978). However, it is likely that triangular arrow points were used in Late Prehistoric times in south Texas. Fresno points are dated to A.D. 1440-1760 at the Tortuga Flat site (41 ZV 155) in Zavala County. The type has also been found with late burials at the Unland site in Cameron County (Robert J. Mallouf, personal communication).

GUERRERO   These arrow points, triangular to lanceolate in shape, are Historic in age and were made in the Spanish missions of Coahuila and Texas. They represent the survival of chipped stone technology among the missionized Indians of south Texas and northeastern Mexico (Hester 1977b; Fox 1979).

HARRELL   Triangular points with either side notches or side-and-basal notching; widely dispersed across much of the United States in Late Prehistoric times. Similar specimens, without basal notches, are termed Washita on the lower Plains. They occur rarely in south Texas.

"LOZENGE"   Lozenge-shaped points described by Corbin (1974) from the central coast north of Corpus Christi; they are in no way related to the lozenge-shaped Desmuke points of Archaic times.

McGLOIN   Triangular points with a convex, V-shaped base; found in the Corpus Christi Bay area.

PADRE   Small, round-based points from the north Padre Island-Corpus Christi area.

PERDIZ   Along with Scallorn, these are the most common arrow points in south Texas. They are often found in sites associated with bone-tempered pottery and bison remains. Radiocarbon dates for Perdiz in the region range from A.D. 1370 at the Hinojosa site (41 JW 8) near Alice in Jim Wells County (Hester 1977c) to possibly as late as the mid-eighteenth century at 41 ZV 155, Zavala County. A date of A.D. 1530 is associated with Perdiz points at site 41 BX 36 in northern Bexar County. The so-called Cliffton points are probably unfinished or poorly made Perdiz points.

SCALLORN As noted above, this is a common type. In central Texas, Scallorn dates around A.D. 700-900 and is earlier than Perdiz. However, in south Texas, this may not be the case, as the types seem to co-occur at some Late Prehistoric sites. There are regional variants of Scallorn, including a series of specimens from McMullen County with deep serrations (small notches) on the edges of the point.

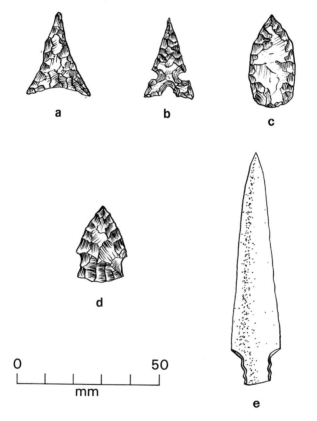

Figure 5.11. **Major Arrow Point Types**. a, Starr; b, Toyah; c, Young; d, Zavala; e, metal arrow point of Historic period.

Figure 5.11

STARR This type is found in the lower Rio Grande Valley, on both sides of the Rio Grande, and also extending up the coast to near Baffin Bay. There are no direct radiocarbon dates for the type, but it is present in the Brownsville Complex.

TOYAH   Somewhat similar to Harrell, but smaller and more crudely made. They are occasionally found in south Texas and may have persisted into early Historic times.

YOUNG   This arrow point type has a generalized round-based form, and some specimens may actually be arrow point preforms. Similar specimens occur in south Texas, both on the interior and on the central coast.

ZAVALA   These are thick, stubby points made much like dart points. However, they are found in Late Prehistoric sites, co-occurring with the thin, light arrow points, and have been dated as late as A.D. 1650. They are suggested here to have functioned as arrow points.

METAL ARROW POINTS   Although not part of the chipped stone industry, it is appropriate to note this arrow point form here. They are, of course, Historic, and were used by Comanche, Lipan Apache, Tonkawa, and others who roamed the area in the eighteenth and nineteenth centuries. Specimens have been found at several sites in south Texas. The most common form has a long, narrow blade and a rectangular stem with notching on both edges.

SHELL ARROW POINTS   As with metal points, it seems best to note these artifacts here. They are generally triangular, chipped from clam shell (the Sunray Clam) and have been reported from sites around Corpus Christi and Baffin Bay. Another shell arrow point form, bullet-shaped and fashioned from the columella of the Gulf conch, is found in the Brownsville Complex in the Rio Grande Delta (Fig. 5.20).

TOOLS

Most tool forms are not characterized by the standardization seen in point types. Thus, there is no "quick reference" to these, as we have with Suhm and Jelks for projectile points. Some of the best known tools forms—both unifacial and bifacial—are described here.

KNIVES (Fig. 5.12).   Thin bifaces, usually triangular, with sharp acute-angled edges. It is often difficult, without benefit of microscopic examination, to distinguish knives from preforms. Often, knives in south Texas are very finely-flaked, finished by pressure-

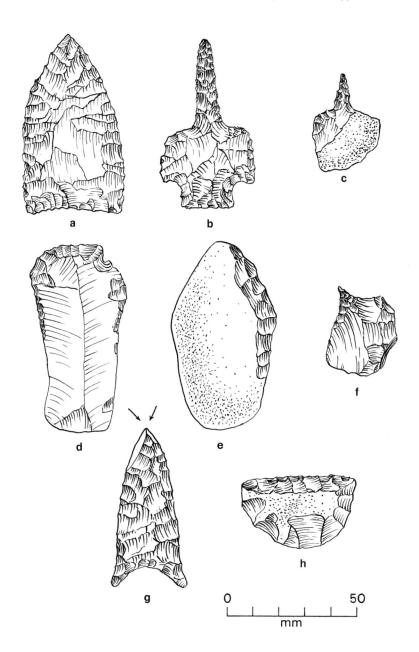

Figure 5.12. **Chipped Stone Artifacts**. a, knife (thin biface); b, drill or perforator, Archaic period; c, drill or perforator, Late Prehistoric period; d, end scraper; e, side scraper; f, graver; g, burin (burins on a point; arrows indicate direction of burin blows); h, Nueces scraper.

flaking, and the edges are dulled or polished from use. Knives were probably hafted on short handles, as are the specimens found at Cueva de la Candelaria in southwestern Coahuila. In the Late Prehistoric, diamond-shaped, bevel-edged knives are often found associated with Perdiz points, bone-tempered pottery, and bison remains (Hester and Hill 1975).

PERFORATORS (Fig. 5.12). Perforators or drills have long, narrow shafts or bits, probably used in working wood, shell, and hide. The tips are often blunted or dulled from such use. In Archaic times, the drills are usually large bifaces, sometimes made on broken dart points (or, at least they have typical dart point stems!). It is assumed that they were hafted. In the Late Prehistoric, perforators are smaller, usually unifacial, and made on flakes.

SCRAPERS (Fig. 5.12). There are a wide variety of unifacially-flaked artifacts throughout south Texas and most probably functioned as scrapers. Most specimens were probably hafted for use (Fig. 5.15). We have to be cautious in labeling all unifaces as scrapers; microscopic study of edge wear has shown that some were actually used as knives or cutting tools. Scrapers are found in a wide range of shapes and forms, but most are characterized by a steeply-flaked working edge. The various kinds of scrapers include end scrapers (particularly common in the Late Prehistoric period), side scrapers (a scraping edge is found along one or both sides of the flake), convergent scrapers (scraping edges meeting in a pointed fashion) and so forth. (See Hester, White, and White 1969 for further descriptions of south Texas scraper forms.)

There are some area-specific scraper forms, and one of these, called the Nueces scraper, has been described by Hester, White, and White (1969: 148). These specimens are bifacial; they range from crescentic to trapezoidal in outline, and have a steeply-beveled bit at the widest end. Nueces scrapers appear to be most common along the middle Nueces River and the lower Frio River in McMullen and LaSalle Counties. A few have been found in Dimmit and Zavala Counties.

GRAVERS AND BURINS (Fig. 5.12). These tool are generally made on flakes. Gravers have small, carefully-chipped protrusions or beaks, used in cutting or engraving. Burins are specialized

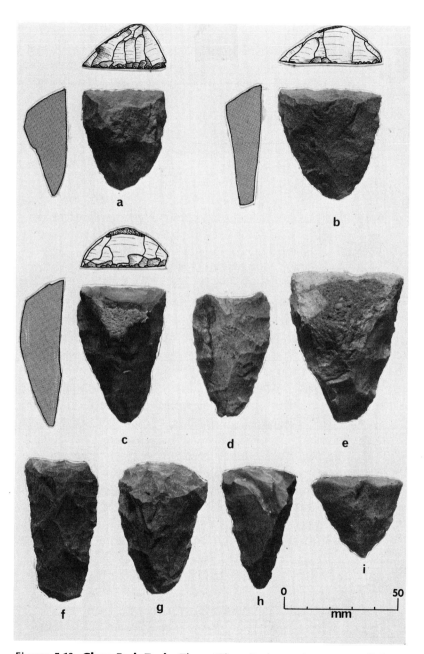

Figure 5.13. Clear Fork Tools. These Clear Fork specimens are all from Dimmit County. Cross-sections and views of bits or working edges are shown for a-c.

tools created by the removal of long, narrow flakes to form a chisel-like edge ideal for gouging, engraving, and cutting. Sometimes burins are made on broken projectile points. Usually a professional archaeologist will have to aid you in identifying a burin artifact; specialized publications, such as Pitzer (1977) will help.

CLEAR FORK TOOLS (Fig. 5.13). Clear Fork tools or "gouges" are very common in south Texas. They are sometimes referred to as "turtlebacks" because of their pyramidal plano-convex cross sections. Their high frequency on south Texas sites indicates that they were a commonly used tool, principally in Archaic times. Hester, Gilbow, and Albee (1973) have done microscopic wear-pattern studies of Clear Fork tools and suggest that they were principally used in woodworking activities.

In Paleo-Indian times, the Clear Fork tools are long, parallel-edged bifaces. During the Pre-Archaic, at least in south-central Texas, they are large unifacial forms. Throughout the Archaic in south Texas, they are usually 5 to 9 cm long and are unifacial. The working end or bit is steep; on some variants the bit edge is concave or even convex, but they are most commonly straight. It is likely that some (if not all) Clear Fork tools were hafted in wooden handles. The author has seen traces of asphaltum on the pointed ends (opposite the bit) of some Victoria County specimens. This suggests one method of binding the specimens in a haft.

In Dimmit, Zavala, and nearby interior counties, a gray quartzite—a very durable, hard stone—was usually selected for the manufacture of Clear Fork tools during the Archaic. Often, there are sites with clusters of Clear Fork tools, suggesting specific work areas. At 41 ZV 109 (Chaparrosa Ranch), numerous Clear Fork tools were found on the top of a gravel hill, away from an occupation site. This may represent a site in which Clear Fork tools were used in a special activity. One has to be wary, though, of groups of these tools on surface sites. Some relic-collectors will pick them up, even stack them up, during collecting episodes at a site, thus creating an artificial clustering.

GUADALUPE TOOLS (Fig. 5.14). The Guadalupe tool is not especially common in south Texas, although specimens are sometimes found in intensive surveys (such as the UTSA Choke Canyon

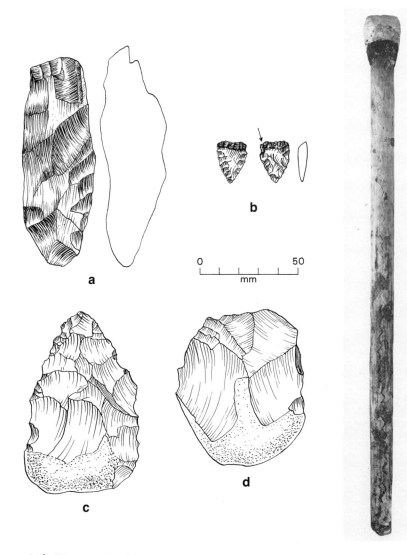

Left, Figure 5.14. **Chipped Stone Artifacts**. a, Guadalupe tool (cross section shown); b, Olmos tool (both faces and cross section shown; on left, specimen has resharpening flakes removed from bit; at right, a burin has been formed, as indicated by arrow, on one corner of bevel-edged bit); c, core-chopper; d, core (bifacial).

Right, Figure 5.15. **Hafted Scraper from Northeastern Mexico**. Small unifacial scraper hafted with pitch at the end of wooden handle; note incised decorations on handle. Length of specimen is 39.1 cm. From a burial cave in southwestern Coahuila (see Hester 1971b).

research near Three Rivers). They are more frequent along the middle and lower drainages of the San Antonio and Guadalupe Rivers. The tools are quite distinctive: they have a triangular cross section, a long, crudely-flaked body, and an oblique-angled bit. We have no idea how these tools were used. They are sometimes called "adzes" or "gouges", but there is no wear-pattern evidence on the bit edges to support either interpretation. Excavations in south-central Texas clearly indicate that Guadalupe tools date to Pre-Archaic times.

OLMOS TOOLS (Fig. 5.14). The Olmos tool (or "Olmos biface") is a highly distinctive little triangular tool. They are found mainly along the drainage system of Los Olmos Creek, which runs from west of Laredo into Baffin Bay. The tools are especially common in the Baffin and Grullo Bays area near Kingsville, and also along the Los Olmos in Duval County. Typically, the bit is much resharpened and there are usually burins on the corners of the bit. Shafer and Hester (1971) suggest they may have functioned as scrapers and that they date to Late Archaic (and possibly Late Prehistoric) times. They would have to have been hafted for use.

CHOPPERS (Fig. 5.14). Choppers are generally large and crude, with an edge formed by large percussion flakes at one end of a cobble; the opposite end, which would have been grasped in the hand, is covered with cortex. Battering and dulling of the chopping edge are indicative of heavy wear, perhaps in woodworking, heavy butchering, or processing plant foods. It is easy to confuse choppers with cores (see below). Further compounding that problem is the fact that abandoned or exhausted (used up) cores were often reused as choppers ("core-choppers" in the archaeological literature).

CORES (Fig. 5.14). These are not tools per se, although they sometimes saw secondary use as choppers or hammerstones. Cores are produced by flake removals in the lithic reduction process described earlier in this volume. A discussion of south Texas core types is found in Hester (1975) and Lynn, Fox, and O'Malley (1977).

GROUND STONE ARTIFACTS

Implements and artifacts of ground and pecked stone in south Texas are rather limited in variety. Most common are handstones or *manos* made of sandstone, quartzite or other stone. These were used to grind and process wild plant foods on a grinding slab or *metate*. The metate is usually of sandstone and may have one or more grinding facets on one or both sides of the slab. Most manos and metates date to the Archaic, but continue into the Late Prehistoric. In some sandstone outcrops in southern Texas, one can see "bedrock metates", shallow grinding depressions in the bedrock. One notable site is 41 WB 58 overlooking the Rio Grande in Webb County.

Pestles, which are long, cylindrical, rounded pounding tools for plant food processing, are also known from south Texas but are very rare. Large stone mortars (in which such pestles were often used in other parts of North America, particularly in the Desert West) are absent. These stone pestles may have been used in wooden mortars, of the type reported for the general region by the Spanish. Such wooden mortars have long since decayed; however, Collins and Hester (1968) report a wooden mortar and a wooden pestle preserved in a dry cave in southwest Texas.

Another type of ground stone artifact is the *stone smoking pipe*. These large, barrel-shaped artifacts are found in the south Texas Archaic, although some may have been used in the Late Prehistoric. Specimens have been found at occupation sites and in cemetery sites. One specimen, with a bone stem still in place, was found in a burial site on Grullo Bay near Kingsville. At site 41 LK 28 near Three Rivers, a number of these pipes were found associated with burials (Fig. 5.16).

Artifacts of incised and grooved sandstone or limestone have also been reported. Irregular pieces of sandstone often have deep, V-shaped grooves cut at various angles on one face. These may result from the use of the abrasive sandstone for smoothing the edges of bifaces during the tool-making process; others may have been used in shaping and polishing bone tools, such as awls.

Incised and grooved limestone artifacts are more common on the fringes of the southern Edwards Plateau. Specimens are oblong and usually have a group of three or more incised lines running parallel along the long axis of the stone. Sometimes there is a deep groove

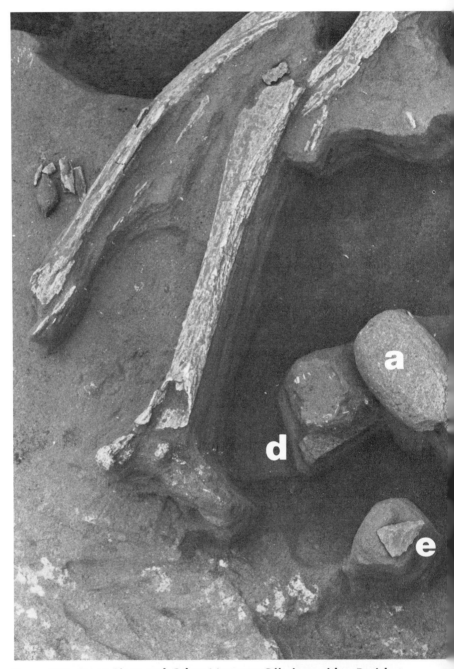

Figure 5.16. **Stone Pipes and Other Mortuary Offerings with a Burial at Site 41 LK 28**. a, stone pipe (note bone mouthpiece); b, bone awls; c, stone

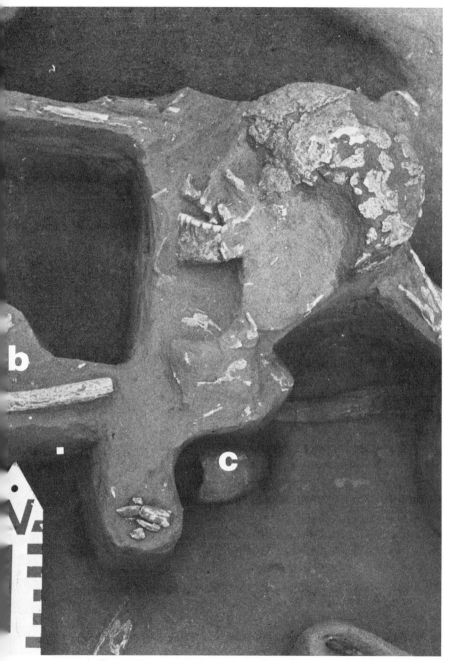

pipe; d, flint knife; e, triangular projectile point. (Photograph courtesy of Charles Johnson II.)

near the center of the stone, perpendicular to the incised lines (see Fig. 5.17). It is thought that these artifacts may have been heated and used as shaft straighteners. Similar artifacts in California were used for straightening cane arrow shafts (Kroeber 1925: 530).

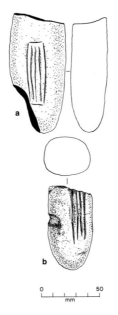

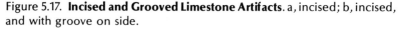

Figure 5.17. **Incised and Grooved Limestone Artifacts**. a, incised; b, incised, and with groove on side.

There are several other kinds of ground stone artifacts that are occasionally found in south Texas. *Boatstones* and other grooved stone objects were probably weights attached to spearthrowers (Fig. 5.18). Such weights might have helped to balance the spearthrower or to give more impetus to the cast of the spear. Experimental studies using spearthrower replicas with boatstones or other weights attached have so far proved inconclusive.

Other ground and polished stones are sometimes notched or notched and grooved. These look like *sinkers* but their function remains uncertain. Some are oval and fully grooved; it has been suggested that they might have been used in the fashion of bolas-weights, attached to cords for the purpose of ensnaring animals. They certainly seem to have been too finely made for use as a net weight. Some examples of these grooved and notched stone artifacts are shown in Fig. 5.18.

Figure 5.18. **Ground Stone Artifacts**. a, boatstone; b, boatstone fragment; c-f, sinker-like artifacts, elongate and oval forms.

Finally, from Victoria County come a series of *faceted quartzite pebbles*. These are oval pebbles of purple-to-reddish-brown quartzite. One or both sides will have one or more facets—small areas where abrading or some other form of use has created a smooth, noticeable depression. Dr. Harry Shafer has suggested that the artifacts might have been used in stone-tool-making, perhaps to scrub the edge of a biface during the thinning process. Illustrations of these unusual artifacts are provided in Chadderdon (1976).

Ground stone *ornaments* are occasionally found. These include beads, both tubular and disc-shaped, made from local and imported stones (such as the jadeite tubular bead from the Floyd Morris site in Cameron County). There are also flat, oval "gorgets" of limestone, slate, or schist, with two perforations and sometimes with notching of the edges or some other form of decoration. Pendants of stone have been found, with a hole or perforation at one end. Most of the ground stone ornaments appear to be from the Archaic period.

BONE AND ANTLER ARTIFACTS

Not many bone and antler artifacts are preserved in the open occupation sites of south Texas. When they are found, they consist of such forms as *bone awls* (made on splinters of mammal long bone or from a deer ulna), *bone pressure-flaking tools* (usually made on a deer ulna; Fig. 5.19), *bone beads* (made of sections of bird, mammal, or even human long bones; Fig. 5.19), and *tiny bone needles* (often with an eye at one end). Occasionally bone awls are found with coastal burials, decorated with incised lines that are sometimes filled with asphaltum.

The most common antler artifact is the *tine pressure-flaker*, made from the tine end of a whitetail deer antler and usually showing wear from use at the tip. Small *billets* (for careful percussion flaking), made of the lower cylindrical sections of deer antler, are less common.

SHELL ARTIFACTS

There are two sources of raw material for shell artifacts in south Texas: the river mussel from muddy stream bottoms, or marine shell that had to be obtained (probably through trade) from the Gulf Coast. Mussel shell artifacts are very fragile. The most common types

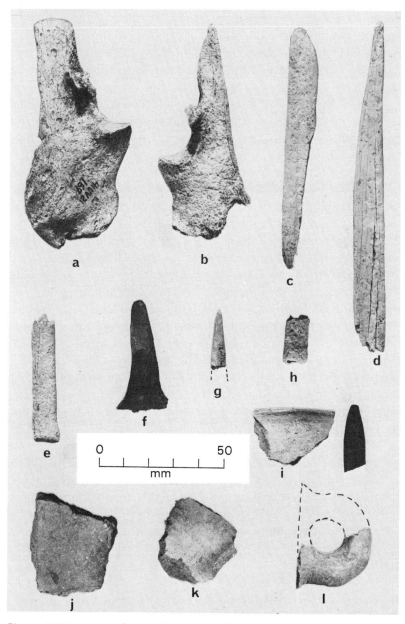

Figure 5.19. **Bone, Antler, and Pottery Artifacts**. All specimens are from the La Jita site in Uvalde County: a, b, flaking tools made on deer ulnae; c-e, bone awls made on splinters of deer bone (all are fragments); f, g, tips of deer antler, probably fragments of flaking tools; h, bone bead; i-l, pieces of bone-tempered pottery (i is a rim fragment; l, a handle).

are small, square, or rectangular beads. Occasionally, mussel shells will be decorated with drilled-dot or punctate designs on the interior, or will have perforations drilled through them. Conch and clam shell artifacts are found in the interior, usually consisting of disc-shaped beads or rectangular pendants.

On the coast, shell artifacts were used extensively for both utility and ornament. Utilitarian artifacts included points made of clam and conch shell (see above), and adzes or scrapers made of conch, clam, and cockle shell. Large conchs or whelks were also sometimes used as hammers. Extensive use of conch was made in the Aransas Phase of the Archaic above Corpus Christi. Adzes and gouges were made of conch shell (Fig. 5.20), and large conchs bear evidence of use as hammers or bashing tools (Fig. 5.20). In Late Prehistoric times, Sunray Clams were often used as scrapers; edges show extensive wear, sometimes chipped for resharpening purposes (Fig. 5.20).

The most extensive use of shell in south Texas was in the Late Prehistoric Brownsville Complex. A massive shell ornament production system was developed, making beads, "tinklers" (sometimes with a coyote tooth suspended inside as a clapper), and pendants or gorgets. Conch shell was heavily used, and occasionally the oval *Dosinia discus* clam (Fig. 5.20) and the olive shell, *Oliva sayana*.

Apparently the Brownsville Complex peoples were producing more shell ornaments than could be used locally. It has been speculated that they engaged in widespread trade—particularly with the Mesoamerican cultures of the Huasteca along the Gulf coast of Mexico (receiving in return pottery, jadeite, and obsidian, which occasionally is found in Rio Grande Delta sites). The trade may have extended to the desert peoples of northeastern Mexico; large numbers of shell artifacts reminiscent of the Brownsville Complex were found in the Cueva de la Candelaria mortuary cave in southwest Coahuila. For more on the shell industry of the Brownsville Complex, see MacNeish (1958), Collins, Hester, and Weir (1969), and Hester (1969b).

POTTERY

At the time of the publication of the *Handbook of Texas Archeology* in 1954, it was believed that the native peoples in the interior of south Texas ". . . remained without agriculture or pottery until they were

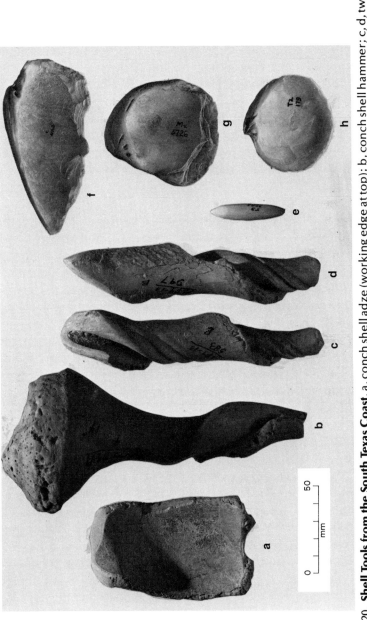
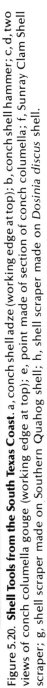

Figure 5.20. **Shell Tools from the South Texas Coast.** a, conch shell adze (working edge at top); b, conch shell hammer; c, d, two views of conch columella gouge (working edge at top); e, point made of section of conch columella; f, Sunray Clam Shell scraper; g, shell scraper made on Southern Quahog shell; h, shell scraper made on *Dosinia discus* shell.

taught these arts by the Spanish friars" (Suhm, Krieger, and Jelks 1954:142). However, very little archaeological work had been done in the region at that time. The intensified research carried out in the past fifteen years has not produced any information to dispute their conclusion regarding agriculture, but it has been clearly established that pottery *was* being made in south Texas in late prehistoric times.

Well over 100 prehistoric pottery-bearing sites have been documented, some yielding more than 1,000 pottery sherds or fragments. At most sites, however, only a few sherds are found. Hester and Hill (1971a) have summarized much of the data on prehistoric pottery in south Texas.

The main ceramic tradition in the interior of the region is characterized by simple vessel forms (bowls, jars, ollas; Figs. 5.22, 5.23), with most of the vessels undecorated, and the paste of the pottery tempered with crushed animal bone. This "bone-tempered pottery" is often called Leon Plain after a similar pottery tradition in central Texas. Surface colors of the sherds and vessel fragments are usually brown, reddish-brown, or pink, reflecting the way in which the pots were fired. White specks seen on the surface are exposed bits of bone temper which were added to the potter's clay for strength (and to reduce shrinkage) before the vessels were formed and fired. T. C. Hill, Jr., of Crystal City, has conducted extensive experiments that have successfully duplicated the ancient pottery-making techniques of south Texas (Hill 1975).

When Hester and Hill wrote their synthesis of south Texas pottery, the largest samples were from Dimmit, Zavala, and Frio counties. Now we know that bone-tempered pottery occurred as far south as Starr County, in Live Oak and McMullen Counties (over 600 specimens were recovered by the UTSA Choke Canyon Project), in Jim Wells County, and in most other areas of south Texas. It usually occurs as small sherds widely scattered on the surface of Late Prehistoric sites. Loop handles (Figs. 5.19, 5.21) or lug handles are also found, indicating the types of handle forms that were on the complete vessels.

It is clear from excavations that the bone-tempered pottery began to be made sometime after A.D. 1200 and continued to be made into the sixteenth or seventeenth century. Most of the pottery sites also yield Perdiz arrow points. The Spanish do not seem to have recorded pottery among the historic Coahuilteco-speakers (al-

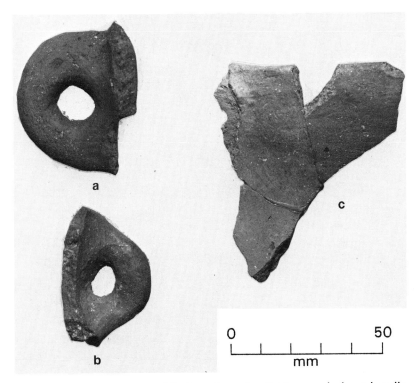

Figure 5.21. **Bone-Tempered Pottery from South Texas.** a, b, loop handle fragments (handles were attached near the vessel rim); c, fragment of vessel, near the rim (white flecks on surface are exposed bits of bone temper).

though it was noted among the Karankawa on the coast); perhaps it was no longer being made at that time. The origins of pottery-making in the region are not clear, but it seems likely that it is derived from central Texas peoples who were making bone-tempered Leon Plain pottery at about the same time.

Another pottery type from the interior of south Texas appears to date largely to the Historic period. This is Goliad ware, defined on the basis of the analysis of 22,000 sherds from the Spanish colonial mission site of Espiritu Santo at Goliad. However, Goliad ware has also been found at other localities in the region. It is sometimes difficult to differentiate it from Leon Plain, but it generally has thicker walls, a darker paste, and two distinctive types of surface decoration. These decorations include the use of asphaltum paint ("black-on-buff") or a rather dull red paint ("red-on-buff") to apply broad

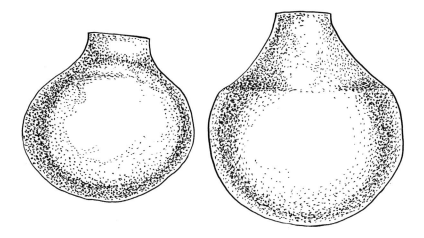

Figure 5.22. **Goliad Ware Vessels from Karnes County.** Sketches of vessels reconstructed from sherds found at the Scarborough site, Karnes County, by C. A. Calhoun. Height of vessels: left, 20 cm; right, 25.5 cm.

straight or wavy lines and small dots to the vessel surface. Other types of decorative techniques noted on Goliad ware include polychrome painting and incised lines. Also, the rims of Goliad pottery are often notched.

As noted above, the initial study of Goliad ware was based on a sample from a mission period collection. Most of the material reported from elsewhere comes from sites that are probably of similar age. It seems likely, therefore, that Goliad ware was being made by mission Indians. The mixing of Karankawa and Coahuilteco Indians at the Goliad missions may have led to the use of asphaltum decoration; red painting may be the influence of the Spaniards. More details on Goliad pottery can be found in Campbell (1961) and Fox and Fitzpatrick (1977; see Fig. 5.23).

Rarely are enough sherds of either Leon Plain or Goliad ware found at a site to allow even partial reconstruction of the pottery vessels. However, C. A. Calhoun of Port Lavaca, Texas, found the fragments of two vessels (olla forms) at a site in Karnes County and was able to reconstruct both of them (see Fig. 5.22). These vessels are probably Goliad ware, but similar ollas were undoubtedly part of the Leon Plain tradition.

Pottery is more commonly found along the south Texas coast. On the coast, the pottery has a sandy feel and appearance. The sherds are gray-colored and thin. Vessels were sometimes decorated with

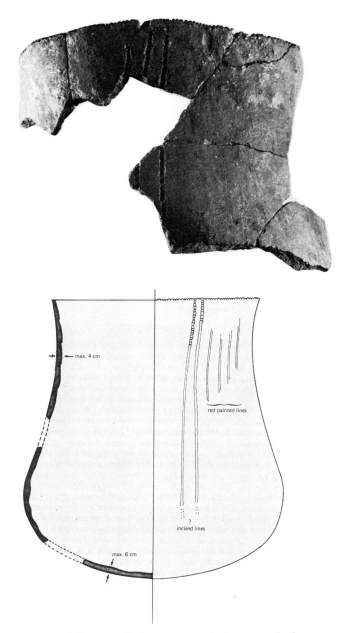

Figure 5.23. **Vessel from Goliad County.** Goliad ware polychrome vessel. Upper, portion of vessel rim (note notching of rim and incised lines perpendicular to rim); lower, artist's reconstruction of vessel, based on available fragments. Approximate height of reconstructed vessel, 19 cm. (Illustrations courtesy of UTSA Center for Archaeological Research and Anne Fox.)

lines and zigzags of asphaltum. This pottery is known as Rockport ware, with the decorated specimens termed Rockport Black-on-Gray. One polychrome vase of this ware has been found on Oso Creek near Corpus Christi. Other decorative techniques include incising and punctations. The motifs painted on the vessels are usually wavy or zigzag lines. The interiors of some pots were covered with asphaltum, apparently as waterproofing.

Rockport pottery is found at sites on the coast and on Padre Island from Baffin Bay to Matagorda Bay. It was first made in the Late Prehistoric period, perhaps around A.D. 1200-1400, and continuing into the Historic period. The pottery described by A. S. Gatschet (1891) as being made by the Karankawa in the nineteenth century fits the description of Rockport ware. However, other coastal peoples in the region may have also manufactured this kind of pottery.*

EXOTIC ARTIFACTS

Artifacts not made by the regional inhabitants, and which found their way into the area through trade, are often the focus of much attention. These exotics include Mesoamerican ceramic figurines or figurine heads, artifacts of obsidian, and chipped stone artifacts made of materials not native to the region. One has to be careful when studying such specimens to be sure that a hoax or prank is not involved and that the specimens are not recent discards, perhaps abandoned by tourists. The specimens from known prehistoric context are of particular interest as they represent trade contacts, perhaps trade networks, in prehistoric south Texas.

A number of the obsidian artifacts have been analyzed for the geological source, using the techniques of nuclear chemistry. Two obsidian arrow points from McMullen County are known to be derived from an obsidian source in southwestern New Mexico. Did these points get here through intrusive Indian groups, such as the Apache? Other specimens have been linked to obsidian sources in Mexico and must have reached the area through long-distance trade, probably passing through many intermediary groups. An obsidian point of Paleo-Indian vintage found at the base of Kincaid Rockshelter north of Sabinal (Uvalde County) has been demon-

*Good discussions of Rockport ware are found in Suhm, Krieger, and Jelks (1954), Campbell (1961), Fitzpatrick, Fitzpatrick, and Campbell (1964), and Calhoun (1964).

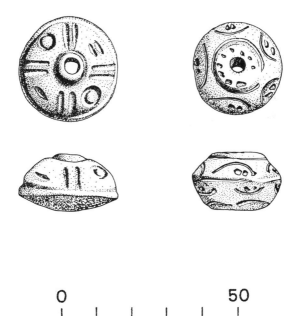

Figure 5.24. **Toltec Period Spindle Whorls from South Texas**. Found on a surface site in Dimmit County (Hester 1972). Top and side views shown for all four specimens.

strated to be from an obsidian source in Queretaro, Mexico, some 600 miles away.

Ceramic figurines, or those made of stone, are sometimes harder to deal with, especially if distinctive features have been eroded away while the specimens lay exposed on a site. One stone figurine, made of serpentine, found in a clay dune in Kenedy County in the late 1940s, appears to be from the Guerrero area of western Mexico. A group of ceramic spindle whorls (weights used in spinning fibers in Mesoamerica) were found at a site in Dimmit County and are derived from the Toltec Culture of central Mexico (Hester 1972; Fig. 5.24). In Bexar County, fragments of pottery from the American Southwest have been found.

Chipped stone artifacts of non-native stones can sometimes be linked to their areas of origin. For instance, at sites in Dimmit and Bexar Counties, some artifacts of the distinctly-colored Alibates dolomite (or "flint") are thought to be from a large quarry on the Canadian River in the Texas Panhandle. Some projectile points seen in south Texas collections are made of dark black chert that probably comes from northeastern Mexico.

Ground stone artifacts typical of central Texas prehistoric cultures are also found in south Texas, especially pendants and gorgets made of limestone, schist, or slate, and notched and grooved pendants of the Waco "sinker" form common to the central Brazos River valley.

6
11,000 YEARS OF SOUTH TEXAS PREHISTORY

Archaeological evidence clearly indicates human occupation in south Texas as early as 11,000 years ago—and maybe earlier. A thorough knowledge of artifacts and sites eventually allows us to reconstruct the culture history of a region. If the cultural periods of south Texas prehistory are still far from fully known, it is because only in the last few years have extensive excavations been carried out and radiocarbon dates obtained. What follows is a summary of present knowledge. Some of it will become outdated before this appears in print; that is the nature of archaeology.

WHAT IS THE EARLIEST EVIDENCE IN SOUTH TEXAS?

There are several localities in south Texas with evidence of habitation attributed to a time prior to 11,000 years ago—that is, before the Clovis Complex (see Chapter 2). For instance, there were claims some decades ago for the association of artifacts and mid-Ice Age fossils in the so-called "equus beds" of Duval County. However, study of an "artifact" from this locale (Hester 1971c) showed that the chipped stone piece found among the fossil animal remains had been worked and weathered by nature.

Friesenhahn Cave, on the border of Comal and Bexar Counties in south-central Texas, is another intriguing situation. Chipped stone pieces from buried zones containing late Ice Age mammals are believed by some archaeologists to be artifacts. Others suggest that the specimens have been modified by nature, not man. Some bone fragments from the deposits also may or may not be artifacts. More specimens have been recovered by recent excavations at this sinkhole cave, but the problem remains unresolved.

Several other localities have yielded strange stone pieces to which some archaeologists would attribute great antiquity. There is Kenneth Honea's "San Marcos Complex" of central Texas and a series of chipped stone objects reported by George F. Carter from the vicinity of Bryan in southeast Texas. Neither case has yet proved to be very ancient.

I do not want to leave the impression that all of these localities say nothing of early human occupation in the southern part of the state. I remain skeptical about them because of the lack of substantial evidence; there are simply no clear-cut data which show convincingly that man was there prior to 11,000 years ago.

There are sites which *might* provide such evidence. For example excavations at the Berger Bluff site (41 GD 30) along Coleto Creek in Goliad County have revealed an occupation zone buried at a depth of 25 feet below the surface. From a small fire-pit in this zone, charcoal was collected and a radiocarbon date of 9600 B.C. was obtained. This is the earliest radiocarbon date for south Texas, and materials from further excavations in late 1979 by The University of Texas at San Antonio should yield more information.

Another site is Bonfire Shelter in Val Verde County, southwest Texas. Excavations by David S. Dibble (Dibble and Lorrain 1967) revealed a "bone bed" (their Bone Bed 1) containing extinct species of bison and possibly mammoth. This was beneath Bone Bed 2, with Folsom and Plainview bison-kill evidence radiocarbon-dated at 8200 B.C. Since Bone Bed 1 was only briefly sampled, we do not know much about it and we do not know its date. The presence of mammoth remains suggests that it may date to Clovis times, or from an even earlier epoch. Similarly, site 41 VV 162, also in Val Verde County, has produced some data suggesting human presence 12,000-14,000 years ago.

At Levi Rockshelter in Travis County, west of Austin, Herbert Alexander has excavated a zone at the bottom of the shelter's deposits which contains identifiable artifacts apparently associated with remains of tapir, dire wolf, and other Ice Age mammals. Again the zone is not directly dated, but it underlies an occupation of 8050 B.C. (Alexander conducted further work at the site in 1977-78.)

Finally, at Montell Rockshelter in Uvalde County, excavations in the late 1940s seemed to produce evidence of the association of artifacts and Ice Age mammals. But on a recent visit to the site the

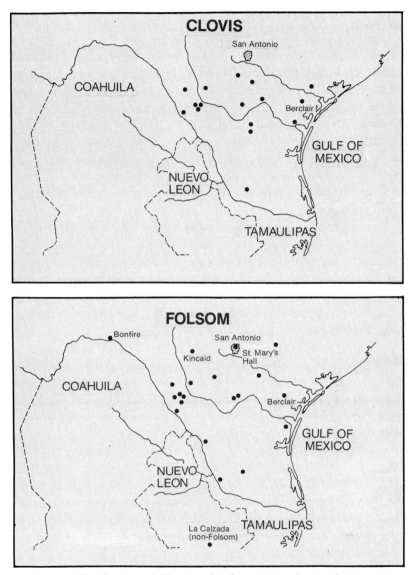

Figure 6.1. **Distribution of Clovis and Folsom Points in South Texas.** Dots represent sites where Clovis (upper) or Folsom (lower) points have been found; at most sites, only one specimen is documented.

author and others found that artifact-looters have so disturbed the deposits that no further work can be done.

PALEO-INDIAN PERIOD

As discussed in Chapter 2, the earliest well-defined period of human habitation in the New World begins around 11,000 years ago (roughly 9000 B.C.), during the waning of the Ice Age or Pleistocene. This marks the beginning of the Paleo-Indian period as we presently know it, continuing until about 6000 B.C.

In the early part of the Paleo-Indian era, around 8000-9000 B.C., there may have been two major cultural traditions in south Texas and adjacent northeastern Mexico. These reflected early human adjustments to differing environments and subsistence resources within the region.

The most visible is the *Plains-related tradition*, in which cultural patterns and technology were derived from, or linked to, Paleo-Indian cultures of the Great Plains and the Southwest. In this I would group all of the Clovis and Folsom occurrences found so far at surface and excavated sites in the region. There is very little evidence, if any, of the presence of Clovis or Folsom points south of the Rio Grande (Fig. 6.1).

Aside from the Bonfire Shelter kill-site in southwest Texas, we have little in the way of faunal associations with Clovis and Folsom materials in south Texas. At Kincaid Rockshelter near Sabinal (Uvalde County), Ice Age bison were found near the bottom of the deposits in a zone where relic-collectors had apparently found several Folsom points. A Folsom occupation site has recently been found in northern San Antonio at site 41 BX 52. Excavated by the Archaeology Section of the Texas Department of Highways and Public Transportation in 1979, the site yielded Folsom points, unfinished Folsoms (preforms), Folsom-type end scrapers (some with characteristic beaks on one corner), and much debris from associated stone tool-making activities. No animal bones were recovered but the presence of a lifeway similar to that of Folsom peoples on the Plains is clear.

A Folsom point was also excavated from an area of the St. Mary's Hall site (41 BX 229). Further exploration showed that the particular area in which it was found had been badly disturbed in ancient times by erosion, and no related fauna were recorded. In Fig. 6.1, the distribution of many of the known Folsom points in south Texas is

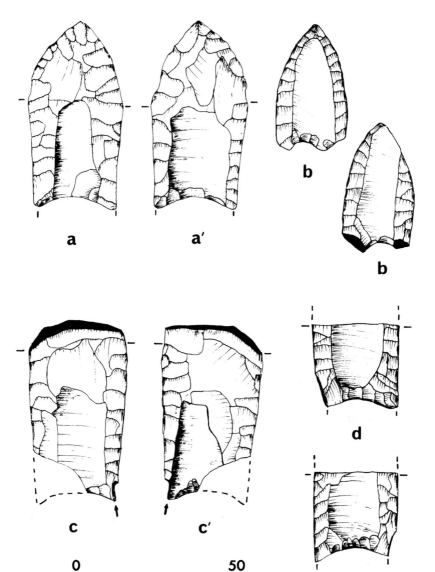

Figure 6.2. **Clovis and Folsom Points from Southern Texas.** Both sides are shown for each specimen. a, a', northwestern Zavala County (Clovis); b, b', northwestern Zavala County (Folsom); c, c', 41 ZV 27, Zavala County (Clovis); d, d', Atascosa County (Clovis).

shown. We assume that all of these materials date sometime around 8800-8500 B.C.

In dealing with the earlier Clovis materials (around 9200 B.C., based on radiocarbon dates from sites in New Mexico and Arizona), we have a similar situation—widely scattered finds of Clovis points. A possible exception is the Buckner Ranch locality (41 BE 2) in Bee County, discussed later in this chapter. Mammoth remains, of the sort found at Clovis kill-sites, are common throughout south Texas. However, most skeletal parts are found as secondary deposits, previously eroded and scattered through stream silts.

Since 1975, geologist Raymond Suhm of Texas A&I University (Kingsville) has excavated the La Paloma locality in Kenedy County (Fig. 6.3). Mammoth, ground sloth, horse, and extinct bison (*Bison antiquus*) were found, but there was no direct association of human tools with any of the remains. Some artifacts were found in backdirt from bulldozer cuts; these cannot be linked to the Ice Age fossils and none of them resemble Clovis or other early Paleo-Indian types. Radiocarbon dates run on the bones range from 6130 to 7880 B.C.; this is very late for such animals and the dates may be in error.

In this same part of the early Paleo-Indian period, there is substantial evidence from northeastern Mexico of a different cultural tradition, one not influenced by happenings on the Plains. This tradition is very important as it gives evidence of early human utilization of the environment of this region in a way clearly distinct from lifeways on the Plains. These finds are the result of work by Jeremiah F. Epstein and his students at The University of Texas at Austin during the 1960s. Epstein has termed this early evidence the *Small Projectile Point Tradition*. He believes that this tradition was long-lived, with its beginnings dated as early as 8600 B.C. at sites like the La Calzada Rockshelter in Nuevo Leon. Fluted points typical of the Plains-related tradition were not found by Epstein and his students.

The geographic extent of the Small Projectile Point Tradition is still uncertain. It seems likely, though, that these two major traditions may have been present in south Texas-northeast Mexico early in the Paleo-Indian period. These reflect regional adaptations to differences in game and in the environmental setting. The Plains-related fluted point tradition apparently reflects a lifeway found across the Plains, the Southwest, and into parts of south Texas. The small point tradition has been documented so far only in northeastern Mexico. We need more research to see if it may also extend into

Figure 6.3. **Excavation of Ice Age Mammals in Southern Texas**. View of excavation of Late Pleistocene mammoth and other mammals at the La Paloma locality in Kenedy County. (Photograph courtesy of Raymond Suhm.)

parts of south and west Texas.

Problems of definition of cultural patterns become more complex during the Late Paleo-Indian period in south Texas. The Ice Age was over. The new environment, much like that of modern times, created new and varied resources set in a changing landscape. Human populations expanded their activities into practically every available habitat and there are indications that the number of people in the region was on the rise.

Still, the earlier ways persisted; many of the same occupation sites continued to be used by these nomadic hunters and gatherers and they continued to use stone-chipping methods and styles which had prevailed in the early part of the period. This period can be recognized as late as about 6500-6000 B.C. in south Texas.

In this region, the Late Paleo-Indian cultural patterns are known primarily from a number of different projectile point types, usually found on eroded surface sites in widely scattered areas. These types include Plainview, Golondrina, Scottsbluff, and Angostura (see Chapter 4). Plainview dates to around 8200 B.C., Golondrina to

7000 B.C., Scottsbluff at 6500 B.C., and Angostura between 6500-6000 B.C.

There are now a number of important Late Paleo-Indian sites recorded in south Texas and adjacent areas. Bison kill-sites of this era, known from the Texas Panhandle, have not yet been discovered in south Texas. However, at Bonfire Shelter in Val Verde County, a Plainview bison-kill occurred around 8200 B.C.

A Plainview occupation site, one of the very few yet found, is located in northern San Antonio. This is the St. Mary's Hall site (41 BX 229) excavated by the Southern Texas Archaeological Association and by students directed by the author (see Hester 1979). The site is perched on a gentle slope atop a high bluff overlooking the broad valley of Salado Creek. The debris left behind by the peoples who made Plainview points—the Plainview Complex—is buried about three feet below the present ground surface, underlying the occupations of later Archaic and Late Prehistoric peoples. Several Plainview point fragments (basal sections of the sort that would be discarded after breakage during a hunt), unfinished Plainviews (preforms), cores, flakes, scrapers, and other artifacts were uncovered. The living area appears to have covered an area about six by eight meters (517 square feet). By carefully plotting the distribution of the discarded tools and other chipped stone materials, it is possible to recognize distinct clusters that might be areas of specific activities, such as a place where initial stone-chipping was done, an area where broken points were discarded (the central occupation area?) and so on.

Only a few animal bones were found, representing bison and deer-sized animals. Given the placement of the site—on an ideal hunting overlook—we can assume the small group of people of this Plainview Complex occupation site used the Salado Creek valley for hunting. There was insufficient charcoal to radiocarbon date this site. However, the points are strikingly similar to those from Bonfire Shelter where a date of about 8200 B.C. was obtained by David S. Dibble. While no identifiable animal bones were recovered in Plainview occupation at St. Mary's Hall, we suspect the favorite prey of these hunters was a now-extinct species of bison—the kind whose bones were found with Plainview points at Bonfire Shelter and at Plainview kill-sites in the Texas Panhandle.

Overlying the Plainview materials at St. Mary's Hall was a scattering of other Late Paleo-Indian artifacts, including a Golondrina point.

The Golondrina type was once thought to be a variant of Plainview, but recent work has shown it is a separate and later form. The type was originally recognized by Johnson (1964) in his excavations at Devil's Mouth, a deep terrace at the mouth of the Devil's River where it joins the Rio Grande. The site yielded numerous Golondrina points as well as other Late Paleo-Indian points. Golondrina could not be fixed as to age at that time. Later, a radiocarbon date linked to Golondrina was obtained at Devil's Mouth, indicating that the type was about 9,000 years old (6830 B.C.).

Further light was shed on Golondrina and the important cultural pattern which it represents by excavations at Baker Cave, also in Val Verde County. The site is a rockshelter in a canyon wall of a Devil's River tributary. The first excavations were by James H. Word, an amateur archaeologist from Floydada, Texas (Word and Douglas 1970); he found Golondrina points at the base of the cave's deep, stratified deposits. Then, in 1976, the author and Robert F. Heizer directed additional excavations at the cave; one of their main goals was to learn more about the lifeway which by now had become known as the Golondrina Complex. Word had obtained two radio-carbon dates of about 7000 B.C. and we obtained two more, firmly fixing the age of the point type and the associated cultural pattern.

Of most significance in the 1976 excavations was the discovery of a Golondrina-period cooking pit, capped with burned rocks and filled with an ashy deposit. All of the pit full was bagged up and taken to the laboratory for analysis. Great numbers of charred seeds and animal bones were recovered, including the remains of sixteen different snake species! The plants indicated that the Ice Age was certainly over and more modern conditions prevailed. However, some of the desert plants found in the area today, such as lechuguilla, were absent. Other plants typical of the Devil's River environs today were common in this 9,000-year-old hearth. These included the Texas walnut, persimmon, prickly pear, and several other plants (see Table 6.1).

Similarly, the animals were those of today, but small animals, including lizards and snakes, were most frequent. The bones of carp and other fish were also common (Table 6.2). Taken as a whole, the information indicates a climate somewhat cooler and a bit more moist than that of present Val Verde County (although it rained 17 inches on us during the work in July, 1976!).

Apparently the Golondrina Complex peoples were broadly

Table 6.1 Plant Remains from the Golondrina Complex Hearth, Baker Cave[1]

Seeds and fruits, in order of abundance:

Scientific Name	Common Name	Approx. Ripening Period[2]
Juglans microcarpa	Texas Black Walnut	Fall (October)
Opuntia spp.	prickly pear	July-September
Diospyros texana	persimmon	mid-late summer
Celtis reticulata	net-leaf sugar hackberry	late summer
Celtis pallida	spiny hackberry	mid-summer
Prosopis glandulosa	honey mesquite	August-September
Quercus spp.[3]	oak	see footnote
Sophora secundiflora	Texas mountain laurel	September
Ungnadia speciosa	Mexican buckeye	October
Setaria lutescins	Plains bristlegrass	-
Vigueria stenoloba	skeleton-leaf goldeneye	-
Mahonia or *Berberis trifoliata*	agarita	June
Vitis arizonica	canyon grape	July-August
Acacia berlandieri	guajillo (acacia)	June-July
Karwinskia humboldtiana	coyotillo	October
Rhus microphylla	littleleaf sumac	May-July

Wood identified from the hearth:

Scientific Name	Common Name
Quercus spp.	oak
Juniperus spp.	juniper
Ungnadia speciosa	Mexican buckeye
Celtis spp.	hackberry
Acacia spp.	guajillo
Platanus occidentalis	sycamore
Prosopis glandulosa	honey mesquite
Larrea tridentata	creosote bush

[1]Identifications of seeds and fruits by Phil Dering (Texas A&M University); woods identified from charcoal samples by Liz Porter (Texas A&M University).

[2]Approximate ripening periods of the listed plants are based on data presented by Robert Vines and on the author's personal observations.

[3]Several kinds of oaks may be represented; leaves of the live oak (*Quercus virginiana*) were identified. Acorns are produced by certain oaks on an annual basis, and by others, biennially.

Table 6.2 Faunal Remains Identified from Golondrina Complex Hearth, Baker Cave[1]

Scientific Name	Common Name
Mammals:	
Urocyon cinereoargentus	gray fox
Lepus californicus	black-tailed jackrabbit
Sylvilagus sp.	cottontail
Citellus variegatus	rock squirrel
Citellus sp.	ground squirrel
Neotoma sp.	pack rat
Thomomys bottae	western pocket gopher
Sigmodon hispidus	hispid cotton rat
Peromyscus sp.	whitefooted mouse
Perognathus sp.	pocket mouse
Dipodomys sp.	kangaroo rat
Onychomys sp.	grasshopper mouse[2]
Fish:	
Carpoides carpio	carp sucker
Cycleptus elongatus	blue sucker
Moxostoma congestum	rod horse sucker
Ictiobus sp.	small mouth buffalo
Micropterus sp.	bass, probably spotted bass
Lepomis sp.	sunfish
Reptiles:	
Sceloporus sp.	blue spiny lizard
Arizona elegans	glossy snake
Elaphe guttata or obsoleta	Great Plains or Texas ratsnake
Gyalopion canum	hook-nosed snake
Hypsiglena torquata	night snake
Lampropeltis getulus	common kingsnake
Lampropeltis mexicana	grey-banded kingsnake
Lampropeltis triangulum	milksnake
Masticophis or Coluber	coachwhip or racer
Pituophis melanoleucus	bullsnake
Rhinocheilus lecontei	longnosed snake
Salvadora sp.	patch-nosed snake
Sonora semiannulata	ground snake
Tantilla or Diadophis punctatus	blackheaded or ringneck snake
Thamnophis proximus	ribbon snake
Crotalus atrox	western diamondback rattlesnake
Crotalus molossus	blacktailed rattlesnake
Crotalus sp.	rattlesnake

[1]From 1 to 3 individuals represented in each species; this is only a partial inventory of fauna from the hearth fill as much of the fill remains to be processed. Identifications by Kenneth J. Lord.

[2]Identification of this mammal species and of all of the reptile species is the work of Thomas Van Devender.

exploiting most resources the environment had to offer. They had become gatherers—oriented largely toward food-collecting—and the emphasis on hunting of earlier millenia appears to have disappeared. Artifacts frc n the Golondrina zone at Baker Cave included the typical points, cutting tools, a gouge-like biface stained with red matter, and a host of other tools and debris (see Fig. 6.4).

Epstein, during his work in northeastern Mexico, found a major site of the Golondrina Complex about halfway between Monterrey and Reynosa in the state of Nuevo Leon. This site, San Isidro, is on the surface, but it yielded many Golondrina points and associated gouge-like bifaces, apparently an early form of the Clear Fork tool (Fig. 6.5). Other bifaces of this sort occur at Baker Cave and at Johnston-Heller; the form is dated by absolute means only at Baker Cave.

Returning now to south Texas, we can note the occurrence of a number of Golondrina points (and some Plainview specimens) at sites like Johnston-Heller (41 VT 15) (Birmingham and Hester 1976) and Willeke (41 VT 16), both in Victoria County. However, excavations of the early and deeply buried zones at these sites have not yet been carried out.

Most Late Paleo-Indian points in south Texas occur in surface situations, eroded out by sheet-wash and gullying. Often, they are mixed with Archaic remains that have been let down onto the same surface by this erosion. An area along San Miguel Creek in Atascosa and McMullen Counties contains many eroded sites that have produced quite a number of Late Paleo-Indian points (see Hester 1968). These include Plainview, Golondrina, and Angostura (Fig. 6.6). Scottsbluff points, found in the Cody Complex of 6500 B.C. on the Plains, occur more rarely in south Texas, although they have been found in many counties, such as Frio, Live Oak, Dimmit, and Victoria (Fig. 6.6). A number of specimens are reported from the latter county in a paper by Hester and Hill (1971b). There are other Late Paleo-Indian types that are very rarely found in south Texas, such as Milnesand, Meserve, and Midland, and specimens that have not yet been formally classified.

One south Texas site in which a variety of Paleo-Indian materials were found in buried deposits is Buckner Ranch (41 BE 2), also known as Berclair Terrace, on the Bee-Goliad County boundary. It was excavated in the mid 1930s by the Texas Memorial Museum, under the direction of E. H. Sellards (1940). Since that time, the site has been largely ignored. Some archaeologists believed it to be

Figure 6.4. **Artifacts from Baker Cave, Val Verde County.** a, Golondrina basal fragment; b, ventral (lower) face of bifacial Clear Fork tool; note extensive wear that has obliterated flake scars. a, b are from the Golondrina Complex deposits of ca. 7000 B.C. c-f, sandals from Baker Cave, dating after 3000 B.C. Note differing scales for a-b and for c-f.

mixed through ancient erosion and secondary deposition. Others were perplexed by the apparent co-occurrence of a variety of projectile points, including Clovis, Folsom or Midland, Scottsbluff, Angostura, and stemmed forms of possible Archaic age.

In reexamining the published and unpublished data, it seems that

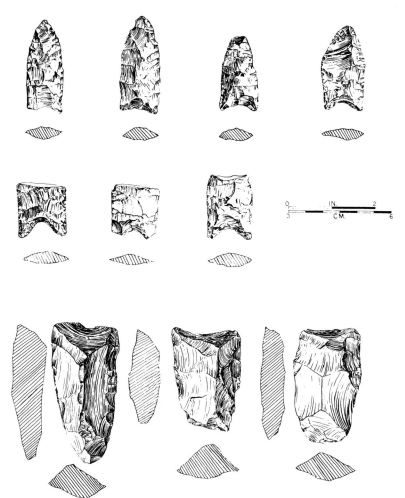

Figure 6.5. **Artifacts from the San Isidro Site, Nuevo Leon**. Upper two rows, Golondrina points; lower row, Clear Fork tools. (Note differing scales). (Illustrations are from Epstein 1969; courtesy of Department of Anthropology, The University of Texas at Austin, and Prof. J. F. Epstein.)

the locality probably served as an occupation site for a succession of Paleo-Indian peoples over a fairly long time period. In addition to the points, there were bones of late Ice Age mammals, an abundance of flakes resulting from tool-making, chipped stone tools (such as the Clear Fork tool), and such oddities as burned mud-

Figure 6.6. **Paleo-Indian Projectile Points from South Texas**. a, b, Folsom points; 41 DM 3, Dimmit County; c, Scottsbluff, Frio County; d, Golondrina; e, Plainview; f, possible Milnesand (d-f, San Miguel Creek; Hester 1968); g, Angostura, 41 VT 15, Victoria County. (Courtesy William Birmingham; sketches of specimens a-c are by Frank A. Weir.)

dauber nests (probably reflecting a food resource—baking the mud-dauber larvae) that we do not often think of in connection with these early sites.

Sellards' excavation techniques were adequate and he was aided by an excellent geologist, Glen L. Evans. His recording methods from the horizontal perspective were quite good; perhaps confusion about the site has arisen because of the inadequate (by modern standards) vertical controls which obscured changes through time. For example, the artifacts and materials mentioned above occurred in the Lower Horizon at Buckner Ranch, and this was a five-foot-thick zone! Depths were recorded for the points, but only in relation to surface datum points which did not take into account possible subsurface undulations of buried strata.

What may have occurred at Buckner Ranch in the Paleo-Indian period was the reuse of a favored occupation site to which mobile groups returned on an occasional basis over a period of perhaps 2,000-3,000 years. As to the presence of notched and stemmed points which look "Archaic", we have learned in recent years that some stemmed points were being used in Late Paleo-Indian times in Texas.

By 6000 B.C., human populations had increased considerably in south Texas. The environment had further modified, perhaps becoming somewhat drier and warmer about this time or shortly after. Hunting and gathering continued as the way of life, with the latter probably dominant. The patterns of Paleo-Indian life styles began to break down in fairly rapid fashion and a new era in the prehistory of south Texas—the Archaic—was developing.

PRE-ARCHAIC PERIOD

This period, between 6000-3500 B.C., represents the transition between Paleo-Indian and developed Archaic lifeways. We still know very little about this epoch. It appears that some aspects of Paleo-Indian stone-chipping continue, especially careful flaking on points. Sites are often located where Paleo-Indian peoples had once camped. The climate may have undergone a period of warmer and more arid times, known as the Altithermal in the western United States. For the present, we can say simply that some kind of transition phase occurred and that it is characterized by distinctive artifact styles. Most evidence so far, in terms of stratigraphy and dating, has come from sites in central and southwest Texas. In central Texas, much information has been obtained from Jetta Court (Travis County) and Stillhouse Hollow (Bell County), and at La Jita, a site just outside Utopia in northern Uvalde County (Fig. 6.7). In southwest Texas, these sites include Devils' Mouth and Baker Cave (with a date of 6100 B.C. from the latter for the early part of the period).

The typical artifacts include Early Corner Notched and Early Triangular dart points, large-barbed Bell points, and stemmed points called Gower. Two tool forms, a unifacial variety of Clear Fork and the Guadalupe tool, are also found (see Chapter 5).

A site dating to this early cultural phase has been found on Salado Creek in San Antonio. This is site 41 BX 271 (Granberg II site), part of a much larger Archaic period site destroyed by highway construction in 1963.

The site is buried in a stream terrace, and excavations in 1974 and 1979 revealed deposits up to ten feet deep. The top 55 cm of these deposits (Stratum II; Stratum I is recent fill) can be described as a "burned rock midden" (gray-black ashy midden soil with an abundance of burned rock and occupational debris). Diagnostic artifacts from this upper unit date from the Late and Middle Archaic periods. At a depth of 55-60 cm, Stratum III occurred as a ten- to fifteen-cm "transitional" zone, with burned rock and ash-stained midden soil grading into gravel. Pedernales dart points were found at the top of the zone, lying on the contact with the overlying burned rock midden.

Beginning at approximately 60 cm and continuing to a depth of 3.60 meters there was an alluvial gravel deposit in which eight strata were recognized. Stratum IV consisted of small gravels in yellow-red clay matrix; burned rocks and lithic materials were found. This stratum produced most of the diagnostic tools. These included several styles of dart points such as Bell, the Early Corner Notched and Early Triangular, Gower, several corner-notched points, numerous large, unifacial Clear Fork tools, a number of Guadalupe tools, preforms, cores, and much lithic refuse. A radiocarbon date of 3400-3600 B.C. was obtained from this stratum in 1979. Stratum V was distinguished by coarse gravels and was 75 cm thick. Stratum VI was composed of fine sand and mixed small gravels and was about 25 cm thick. Stratum VII was also marked by fine sand, but with small gravels, many of which appear crushed. Stratum VIII was a very compact, charcoal-stained zone about 10 cm thick. Part of a distinct living floor was exposed, beginning at about 2.45 meters and sloping

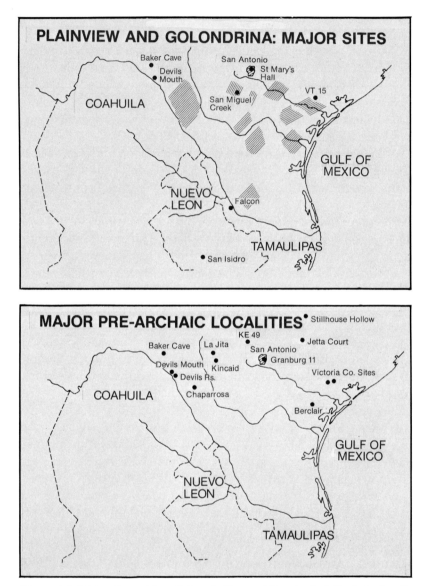

Figure 6.7. **Major Sites of Late Paleo-Indian and Pre-Archaic Periods, South Texas**. Upper, locations of sites with Plainview and Golondrina artifacts; shaded areas indicate the presence of several sites with these materials in a particular area. Lower, locations of sites with Pre-Archaic remains.

upward to roughly 2.30 meters in adjacent units. On this floor were lithic materials, snail shells, some burned rocks, and several Guadalupe tools—four found in an apparent cache. Some of the flakes found here seem to be related to the Guadalupe manufacturing process. Stratum IX was composed of fine sorted gravels, 0.5 to 3 cm in diameter. Stratum X consisted of sandy clay with some gravels. Stratum XI was the deepest stratigraphic unit that was revealed and was composed of large, heavy gravels. A chert core was found in this stratum. It exhibited sharp edges and showed no evidence of having been stream-rolled. This specimen was the deepest object of definite human manufacture.

Other examples of this Pre-Archaic horizon are scattered across southern and south central Texas at sites such as 41 KE 49 (Kendall County) and 41 VT 17 (Victoria County) and at sites on Chaparrosa Ranch, Zavala County.

ARCHAIC PERIOD

The anthropologist Carleton S. Coon has estimated that no more than .003 percent of today's human population makes a living through hunting and gathering. Ten thousand years ago, prior to the development of agriculture and animal husbandry, 100% of the world's population followed the hunting and gathering way of life. In fact, of man's known time span on the earth—an estimated 4 million years—99% of it has been spent in the pursuit of animals and the gathering of wild plant foods.

No single period epitomizes the hunting and gathering lifeway more than the Archaic. To be sure, the earlier peoples in southern Texas, of Paleo-Indian and Pre-Archaic times, followed a similar lifestyle. But during the Archaic, this mode of existence was fine-tuned. Specific technologies were developed for hunting, careful scheduling went into the gathering of wild plant foods and other edibles, the size of the population group and the manner in which it moved around the landscape were controlled by the hunting and gathering subsistence regime. This way of life lasted a long time — from about 5000 B.C. until the advent of Europeans.

Archaeologists studying the Archaic period still do not know exactly what the countryside looked like in southern Texas during these several thousand years. Early European visitors in the Historic period reported grassy plains in much of southern Texas, with heavy tree growth (oaks, elms, etc.) along the rivers and the major creeks.

The infestation of mesquites was to come later. Antelope were seen as far south as Willacy County on the coastal margin; bison roamed over much of the area, recorded south of Eagle Pass in the early 1700s. The rivers and many of the creeks ran year round with water. Was this what it was like during the period from 6000 B.C. until the early 1500s when the first Europeans arrived on the scene?

Probably not. We have found through archaeological research that there may have been climatic fluctuations and changes in the patterns of vegetation and animal life. Ralph Robinson of UTSA has been studying soil samples taken from deeply buried Archaic camp-sites. On the basis of his studies of microscopic particles called phytoliths (see p. 22), he believes there were varying periods of moist and dry conditions as reflected in different grass species. Robinson's work is still tentative at the time of this writing, but as it progresses we will know more about the kinds of plants that were available to the peoples of the Archaic.

Other evidence comes from the identification of plants through the analysis of charcoal left from the campfires of the Archaic peoples. At site 41 LK 31-32 near Three Rivers, UTSA archaeological teams directed by Grant D. Hall excavated several large hearths containing abundant pieces of wood charcoal. Some of the charcoal was used for radiocarbon dating, and this analysis indicated an occupation of Archaic peoples at 3400 B.C. Other pieces of the charcoal from this and other Choke Canyon sites were sent to the Texas A&M Anthropology Laboratories where Kathy Vollman examined the microscopic patterns of the wood. Through her studies, she was able to identify oak, acacia, ash, mesquite, juniper, and spiny hackberry. The presence of mesquite at 1300 B.C. is particularly important, as it indicates the presence of this tree in south Texas for the past 3,000 years. It is possible that mesquite was at that time confined largely to the forested zones along the streams; not until late in the prehistoric period and into the Historic era did climatic and soil conditions create environments which helped the mesquite and other thorny brush spread throughout the south Texas land-scape.

Archaic sites are everywhere in south Texas. This does not reflect large populations during that period, but rather the mobile style of life dictated by hunting and gathering. They had to be in the right place at the right time. The group—perhaps a few families number-ing twenty to forty people—had to make use of their intimate knowledge of the terrain, the seasonality of ripening wild fruits, the places where game was abundant, and so forth. With this knowledge, they planned their daily activities.

We get a glimpse of how this information exchange must have taken place from studies that have been made in recent years of Australian Aborigines and the Bushmen of southern Africa. In these groups, the men go out to hunt and the women and children to collect plant foods, small animals, and to dig up roots. In the evening around the smoky campfires, they talk about what they observed during the day . . . animals using a certain waterhole, a favorite hunting area in which game is now absent, a grove of trees rich in nuts. All of this information is assembled and sorted in their minds to enable them to plan their hunting and gathering activities for the next day and for the days ahead. So must it have been among the Archaic peoples of south Texas.

Along with this went knowledge accumulated since birth and passed along from generation to generation—of when the prickly pear fruit would ripen and where, about the availability of pecans on certain stretches of the rivers, of thickly wooded areas where rats could be caught, of special places suited to the hunting and ambush of whitetail deer, and where good flint could be found for making tools. It was not a haphazard way of life; these were not savages who lived from hand-to-mouth each day. Rather, they were equipped with brains as large as our own and with all the mental processes we possess. And their minds were not cluttered with all the technologies—good and bad—with which we have to contend each day.

The stream valleys of the large creeks and rivers may have defined their territories. Certainly it seems that the archaeological distribution of their occupation sites reflects the need to be close to water. Of course, the streamside environments provided more than water. Within these areas, many resources were closely concentrated . . . nut- and fruit-bearing plants, small animals such as rabbits, lizards, and rats; in the streams were fish, turtles, water snakes, and freshwater clams (mussels). The deer and other larger game had to come through this area to get to water and could be ambushed. The larger Archaic sites seem to be at "preferred" spots where perhaps all of these resources, and those we still have no knowledge of, could be most easily obtained.

Such sites were used over and over again through the thousands of years of the Archaic. Probably they were used at certain times each year, maybe with the change of seasons, but this is only speculation at present. The resources around the preferred campsites, however abundant, would not last very long, and soon the group would have to plan its move up or down the stream to another preferred site. At those times of the year when certain resources were very abundant, the isolated groups must have joined together for times of plant food harvest and accompanying social events.

The countless generations and the numberless groups of hunters and gatherers of Archaic southern Texas left behind a rich archaeological record. The most commonly found artifacts are projectile points. As pointed out in Chapter 5, the bow and arrow was not introduced until around A.D. 1000, so the Archaic peoples made use of the *atlatl* (spearthrower) and short spears tipped with dart points made of flint. These dart points were often triangular in shape, with the edges beveled, giving the point a twisted appearance. (Contrary to relic-collector folklore, this does not make the shaft "spin" while in flight.) This type of projectile point has been named Tortugas. It is widespread over all of south Texas but its time range in the Archaic is still not certain.

There were other dart point styles also in use. Unstemmed, round-based points caled Abasolo and Catan and a smaller triangular point, Matamoros, are also common. Other dart points were the lozenge-shaped Desmuke, the heart-shaped Carrizo, as well as Langtry, Frio, Ensor, and other points with stems (see Chapter 5). Other weapons may have included spears, since large, thin, chipped stone artifacts (sometimes called "spear heads") are occasionally found and may have been used as spear or lance tips. However, most seem to have functioned as knives. No objects that we can safely classify as either axe-heads or tomahawks can be attributed to the Archaic.

Most Archaic sites in south Texas contain many tools. Most people overlook these, thinking that they are unfinished artifacts, but these crudely made artifacts were the everyday implements of the Archaic peoples. The most common tool is the triangular Clear Fork tool, flat on one side and convex (almost pyramid-like) on the other. Other types of chipped stone tools include end and side scrapers, Nueces scrapers, and choppers (see Chapter 5).

Manos (handstones) and metates (grinding slabs) were used for the processing of plant foods and seeds. Hammerstones, often made of a purple-brown quartzite, were used for stone-chipping and for breaking small animal bones, cracking the hulls of nuts, and other bashing tasks.

Perhaps one of the most important tools was an ordinary, sharp-edged flint flake. If a deer had to be skinned and butchered, a man could pick up a flint cobble, knock off several good-sized flakes, and go to work. James E. Corbin (on the faculty at Stephen F. Austin State University) conducted a very interesting experiment along these lines several years ago. Jim took a flint core and, with a hammerstone, removed several flakes. Using only two or three of these, all less than three inches long, he skinned a deer in very short order. During the experiment, he tried to use several chipped stone bifaces (of the sort archaeologists have often called "knives") and found that they did not work well at all for such a task. Similar experiments have been carried out by Lee Patterson of Houston, with the same kind of results.

When archaeologists collect flint flakes from the surface of Archaic sites, or recover them from excavations, the edges are always closely examined in the laboratory. Small chips or nicks along one or more edges indicate that these specimens were used for casual, short-term cutting tasks.

Of course, the Archaic hunters and gatherers of south Texas and northeastern Mexico probably had a number of tools made of wood, but these have not survived. Early Spanish explorers in the area noted the Indians using wooden grinding implements, digging sticks, clubs, and other wooden artifacts, and we can assume that their ancestors did likewise.

While hunting and gathering was undoubtedly the basis of Archaic subsistence, we really have little firm evidence on the kinds of animals hunted or the plant foods that were gathered. Animal bones that have been found include the remains of whitetail deer, tortoise, rabbit, rats, and less commonly, bison. Recent work in the Choke Canyon area may help expand this list. Large land snails (*Rabdotus* species) and river mussels were collected as a food supplement. The presence of wood charcoal representing oak, mesquite, and hackberry indicates that these trees were available for the harvesting of nuts, fruit pods, and berries. The hardy seeds of spiny hackberry are preserved in some Archaic sites.

No archaeological data exists on housing. Dwellings were probably temporary shelters of brush, poles, and hides, leaving no archaeological trace. Hearths, usually built on the ground surface and comprised of cobbles of chert and pieces of sandstone, were used for cooking and food preparation (Fig. 6.8). They may have been the focus of family or group activities, as artifacts, flakes, and other debris are often clustered around them.

Chapter 4 provides details on burial sites of the period. Isolated burials seem to have been the norm, but some cemeteries are known along the coast and one major Archaic cemetery in the interior (41 LK 28) has been excavated.

We still know very little about the history of cultural development in the Archaic period in south Texas and northeastern Mexico. As the number of excavated sites increases, and as we obtain more radio-carbon dates, some of the vague Archaic chronological framework is becoming more visible. The data that are presently available on the region's cultural sequence are summarized in Table 6.3.*

LATE PREHISTORIC PERIOD

Sometime after A.D. 1000, and perhaps as late as A.D. 1300 or 1400, there began to be some changes in the prehistoric cultures of south-ern Texas. The people were still hunters and gatherers, always on the move in search of food. The primary change was the introduc-tion of the bow and arrow. This new weapon probably spread rapidly once it was introduced, since it was much more efficient than the atlatl which had been used in the area for thousands of years. The arrows were tipped with small, thin, and very light flint points of various types; these are found over much of south Texas today.

Common types are Perdiz, Scallorn, Fresno, Zavala, and a series of others (see Chapter 5); most are an inch or less in length. Though they look quite fragile, they were used for all types of hunting activi-ties. They have often been called "bird points" but there is sound evidence that they were used for killing deer, bison, and other large

*While there are large numbers of Archaic sites in south Texas, relatively few have been intensively studied by archaeologists. Some of those for which reports have been published and which the reader might want to examine for more details on the Archaic, include: La Perdida (Starr County; Weir 1956); Oulline (La Salle County; Hester, White, and White 1969); Chaparrosa Ranch sites (Zavala County; Hester 1978); also in Zavala County is the Stewart site of Hester and Hill (1973); sites in McMullen, Live Oak, and Atascosa Counties (Lynn, Fox, and O'Malley 1977; Shafer and Baxter 1975); Cuero Reservoir Archaic sites (DeWitt and Gonzales Counties; Fox et al. 1974); and coastal sites in San Patricio and Aransas Counties (Campbell 1947, 1952; Corbin 1963).

Figure 6.8 **Hearth at Prehistoric South Texas Site.** This oval cooking area or hearth is at a site on Chaparrosa Ranch, Zavala County. It was built, on a flat surface, of cobbles, mainly sandstone, chert, and quartzite.

Table 6.3 General Chronologies for South Texas and Adjacent Areas

	South Texas	South Texas Coast	Lower Pecos	Central Texas	Northeastern Mexico
A.D. 1700	Late Prehistoric	Rockport Complex	Late Prehistoric	Late Prehistoric	Mayran Complex
1500					
1000				Toyah Phase	Catan Complex
500		Brownsville Complex		Austin Phase	
—0—					
B.C. 1000			Late Archaic	Late Archaic	
2000	Archaic	Archaic (Aransas Complex)	Middle Archaic	Middle Archaic	Abasolo Complex
3000					Coahuila Complex?
4000			Early Archaic	Early Archaic	Repelo Complex
5000	Pre-Archaic		Pre-Archaic	Pre-Archaic	
6000	Late Paleo-Indian	Late Paleo-Indian	Late Paleo-Indian	Late Paleo-Indian	Nogales Complex
7000	Golondrina Complex	(rising sea levels)	Golondrina Complex	Golondrina Complex	Golondrina Complex
8000	Plainview			Plainview	
9000	Folsom	Folsom	Folsom	Folsom	Small Projectile
	Clovis	Clovis	Clovis	Clovis?	Point Tradition

game, as well as certain kinds of birds. Human skeletons of the Late Prehistoric period have also been found with arrow points imbedded in them; apparently these were often the cause of death.

There were other new stone tools introduced in Late Prehistoric southern Texas. End scrapers (used in working hide or perhaps even wood) came into use; so did little drills or awls made on flint flakes.

This is also when we begin to see the plain, cream-colored pottery generally known as Leon Plain. This pottery usually took the form of ollas, bowls, and straight-sided jars. It was fairly well made, with the exterior surfaces smoothed and lightly polished (see Fig. 5.21). It was thought by Texas archaeologists as late as the mid-1960s that pottery was completely absent from south Texas, but now many pottery sites have been found throughout the interior. Amateur archaeologists, especially T. C. Hill, Jr., and J. W. House, brought the presence of pottery to the attention of the professionals.

Late Prehistoric sites in the interior of south Texas are occupation sites, generally with concentrated midden deposits ten to fifty centimeters thick. The middens yield large amounts of lithic debris, land snails, mussel shells, scattered hearthstones of sandstone and chert, lumps of baked clay, charcoal, and animal bone remains. In plan, some of the sites tend toward an oval shape, while others are linear, paralleling stream courses.

Distribution of Late Prehistoric settlements follows a predictable pattern. They are concentrated on or near the present channels of large creeks or rivers and on abandoned channels or sloughs. In some cases, Archaic deposits are found to underlie the Late Prehistoric middens. When Late Prehistoric sites are not in the streamside zone, adjacent to the channel, they are found out on the floodplain just back from the channel.

Features and patterns within the late sites are still unclear. Data from excavated or surface-mapped sites indicate the presence of pits (sometimes filled with bone or with ash and baked clay), of workshop areas usually related to tool-making, refuse clusters of snails and mussel shell, and hearths. At two sites, 41 ZV 155 (Hill and Hester 1973) and 41 JW 8 (Hester 1977c), there appear to have been areas used for disposal, as large concentrations of bison, deer, antelope, and other mammalian remains have been found in what may be old erosional cuts in which trash (including bones, potsherds, flakes, and broken points) was thrown.

Chipped stone tools, in addition to the points mentioned previously, also include end and side scrapers, often made on blades (long, parallel-edged flakes). Four-edge, beveled, lozenge-shaped knives, bifacial drills, and perforators or gravers made on small flakes are found in excavated sites.

Analysis of flake debris shows that both percussion and pressure techniques were used. Flakes were used for the manufacture of arrow points, scrapers, perforators, and casual cutting tools. Sometimes, only minimal edge trimming was required to shape an arrow point. A number of blades and exhausted polyhedral blade cores have been found. Some blades were used for making Perdiz and other arrow points, as well as some very small end scrapers; the larger blades were fashioned into end scrapers and other scraping tools. This blade technology is widespread in the south Texas, central Texas, and Texas coastal Late Prehistoric. Perhaps reflecting available lithic resources, the size of the blades, and the tools made on them, vary from region to region (Hester and Shafer 1975).

Ground and polished implements are rare. No milling slabs are reported from the Late Prehistoric and manos are infrequent. Hammerstones are, on the other hand, quite common, and are usually made on small cobbles of purple quartzite. In Zavala County a deeply engraved tubular sandstone pipe was found at one site; at another, a rim fragment of a stone vessel (micaceous schist) was excavated.

We do not yet know if there is a time sequence of arrow point styles in south Texas. In central Texas, arrow points of the Scallorn type precede Perdiz points. However, some south Texas Late Prehistoric sites, such as Berclair (41 GD 4) and Hinojosa (41 JW 8), have yielded only Perdiz points. At some sites in Zavala County, excavations have indicated that two or three arrow point types (Perdiz, Scallorn, and Zavala) were used at the same time. At the Tortuga Flat site (41 ZV 155), triangular arrow points and Scallorn points occurred together in the same Late Prehistoric refuse pit.

One of the most interesting aspects of research in the late prehistory of the region is the faunal information that is beginning to appear. At least forty-one individual species have been identified and the information would indicate that little in the way of potential meat resources was neglected. Large mammals, such as bison, pronghorn, and especially whitetail deer are present. However, judging from frequency of occurrence and the number of individuals present per site, the small mammals (jackrabbit, cottontail rabbit, pack rat, and cotton rat) were apparently a major meat resource.

Fish, birds, turtles, snakes, and lizards also figured prominently in the Late Prehistoric diet. Other food resources included the freshwater mussel and large numbers of land snails.

The only direct evidence of plant food is in the form of hackberry seeds and charred fragments of acorns. However, we know from Spanish documents that the gathering of plant foods was the most important activity in the subsistence of Historic peoples in the region.

It is especially significant that the faunal lists include mammals which are no longer in the region, among them bison and antelope. These species help to support the argument for open—perhaps savannah—vegetational patterns in the Late Prehistoric (see Chapter 2). The javelina or peccary and the armadillo are conspicuous by their absence. Both are considered to be recent intruders into the region, and the faunal data bear this out. Javelina is known, however, from one site on the Frio River in McMullen County, dated around A.D. 1300.

Quail, a popular game bird in the area today, is also absent. These birds are rather easy to trap or snare, so their total absence in the faunal lists must indicate that they were not part of the Late Prehistoric diet. Since these birds favor a brushy habitat, their absence may also reflect savannah conditions.

The faunal tabulations reveal no recognizable preference for any particular localized environment for the hunting (or gathering) of animals. Bison and antelope were certainly more common in the uplands. Deer and many of the small mammals inhabited a variety of closely-spaced environs. The streamside and floodplain zones would have been the habitat of many of the small mammals, rodents, reptiles, and birds. In general, most of the fauna represented in the late sites could have been obtained in the immediate site area or without venturing far from the streamside camps.

If one compares the lists of animals from the northwestern part of south Texas with those from Late Prehistoric and early Historic aboriginal occupations in south-central Texas and the south Texas coast, some immediate differences come to view. For example, at Scorpion Cave (41 ME 7) west of San Antonio (Highley et al. 1978), antelope and jackrabbit are absent, probably reflecting local environmental conditions. Although there is the emphasis on deer and small mammals we saw to the south, there seems to have also been a preference at this site for turtles and birds. The occurrence of Canada goose and greenwing teal is interesting; these are present in the area only during winter migrations. In the Late Prehistoric and Historic fauna from the Kirchmeyer site (41 NU 11) near Corpus Christi, we see that bison and whitetail deer are present, but antelope is not. Swamp rabbit is found along with cottontail. Black bear is also represented, as it is at Scorpion Cave, but absent elsewhere in the south Texas faunal record.

There have been extensive studies of Late Prehistoric sites on the south Texas coast. This research in the coastal strip of southern Texas has led to the recognition of two archaeological complexes dating from Late Prehistoric times. One is the Brownsville Complex of the Rio Grande Delta (see map, page 4). It has material culture dominated by artifacts of shell and a sophisticated shell-working technology (Chapter 5). Point types include Starr and Cameron. The Brownsville Complex appears to have had extensive trade contacts extending down the northern Mexican coast into the Huastecan area and into the desert areas of northeastern Mexico. A distinctive trait of the Brownsville Complex was disposal of the dead in special cemetery sites. However, little is yet known about the settlement and subsistence patterns of this complex (Prewitt 1974).

On the central and south-central Texas coast, we find the Rockport Complex (see map, page 4). Campsites are usually confined to coastal or bay-shore margins. Cemetery or burial sites, some apparently of Rockport age, are also found—especially in the Oso Creek area near Corpus Christi. Artifacts include stemmed arrow points (of Perdiz and other types; see Chapter 5), sandy-paste Rockport ware ceramics, often decorated with asphaltum, and a core-blade technology.

HISTORIC PERIOD

The initial Historic contacts, such as Cabeza de Vaca's trek through the region in the 1520s-1530s, had limited impact on the native peoples; but with the advent of the Spanish missions in the late 1600s and early 1700s, the demise of the south Texas Indian groups begins. For the most part, the Indians did not resist the Spanish, although some fighting did occur, especially in the lower Rio Grande Valley. The Indians were in general peaceful, and many went into the missions curious about this strange new way of life. Others were brought by force into the missions by Spanish military expeditions.

Figure 6.9. **View of Excavations at Mission San Bernardo**. Excavations are underway in this photograph within the living quarters of mission Indians at Mission San Bernardo, near Guerrero, Coahuila. (Photograph courtesy of UTSA Center for Archaeological Research and the Gateway Project.)

At the missions, the Indians were taught Christianity and basic "civilized" skills. They were put to work as laborers in building the mission structures, in farming, and in ranching. Many chose to run away—to try to escape to the old way of life. Sometimes troops were sent after them; at other times, they chose to return on their own, especially when food was scarce or when harassed by the Lipan Apache. The native populations were caught between the Spanish northern frontier and the southerly movement of Comanches and Apaches (see Chapter 3).

Up to the present, few clearly identifiable Indian occupation sites of the Historic era have been found. There have been a few sites at which metal arrow points or glass trade beads have been discovered, but these have not been linked to occupational remains that were also present. It is interesting to note that some sites radiocarbon-dated as late as the mid-1700s in Zavala County yield no evidence of introduced Spanish artifacts. It is likely that as late as the mid-eighteenth century, some south Texas groups had experienced

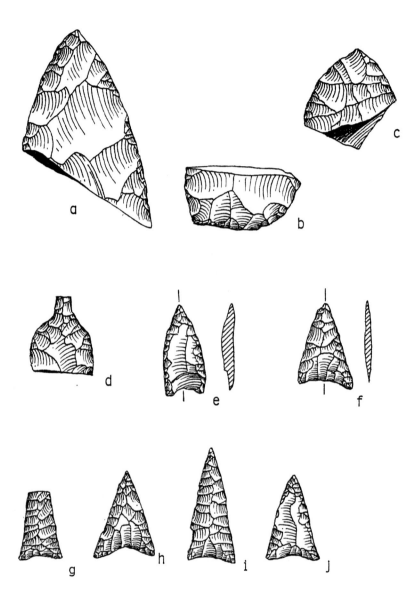

Figure 6.10. **Artifacts of Mission Indians**. a-c, biface fragments, probably pieces of knives; d, drill fragment; e-j, Guerrero arrow points. (From Fox 1979; courtesy of UTSA Center for Archaeological Research.)

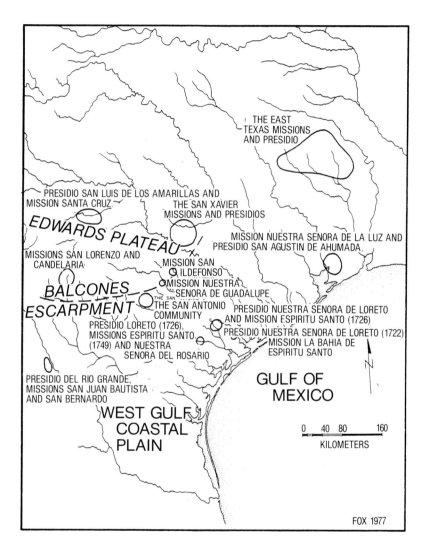

THE EAST
TEXAS MISSIONS
AND PRESIDIO

PRESIDIO SAN LUIS DE LOS AMARILLAS AND
MISSION SANTA CRUZ
THE SAN XAVIER
MISSIONS AND PRESIDIOS

EDWARDS PLATEAU

MISSION NUESTRA SENORA DE LA LUZ AND
PRESIDIO SAN AGUSTIN DE AHUMADA

MISSIONS SAN LORENZO AND
CANDELARIA
MISSION SAN
ILDEFONSO
MISSION NUESTRA
SENORA DE GUADALUPE

BALCONES
ESCARPMENT
THE SAN ANTONIO
COMMUNITY
PRESIDIO NUESTRA SENORA DE LORETO
AND MISSION ESPIRITU SANTO (1726)
PRESIDIO LORETO (1726),
MISSIONS ESPIRITU SANTO
(1749) AND NUESTRA
SENORA DEL ROSARIO
PRESIDIO NUESTRA SENORA DE LORETO (1722)
MISSION LA BAHIA DE
ESPIRITU SANTO

PRESIDIO DEL RIO GRANDE,
MISSIONS SAN JUAN BAUTISTA
AND SAN BERNARDO

GULF OF
MEXICO

N

WEST GULF
COASTAL
PLAIN

0   40   80   160
KILOMETERS

FOX 1977

Figure 6.11. **Locations of Spanish Colonial Missions and Settlements**. (Map by D. E. Fox; from Fox 1979.)

only limited contacts with the Spanish and had not acquired trade goods. Or, if these sites represent Indians who had left the missions, they took little of Spanish manufacture with them. In Zavala County, these might have been Indians from the missions of San Juan Bautisa or San Bernardo at present-day Guerrero, Coahuila.

Most studies of Historic south Texas Indians have been limited to the excavations of their living areas at the various missions (Fig. 6.9). A variety of data come from San Antonio (Schuetz 1969). For example, excavations underway at the time of this writing are revealing new information about the life of the mission Indians at San Antonio de Valero—the Alamo. UTSA archaeologists have been working along the original west wall of the Alamo, now lying beneath rows of stores on Alamo Plaza. A large accumulation of animal bones has been uncovered, representing the food refuse from the Indian living quarters. Mixed among the bones are fragments of Indian pottery, stone tools, and other artifacts. These materials date back into the eighteenth century.

Other excavations have been carried out in the missions around Goliad. At the missions of San Bernardo and San Juan Bautista, near Guerrero, Coahuila, the author and others from UTSA were involved in investigations by the "Gateway Project" in 1975-1977. These missions (Figs. 6.9, 6.10) were located at the "gateway to Spanish Texas", near areas on the Rio Grande where low-water crossings or *pasos* permitted access by the Spanish into what is now Texas. Many of the south Texas Indian groups were residents of these missions. Results of this research project are being published by the UTSA Center for Archaeological Research (see Almaraz 1979; Campbell 1979). In addition, an important study of the stone tools of the mission Indians has been prepared by Daniel Fox (1979) and published by UTSA. The manufacture of stone tools continued to be a trait of south Texas Indians even after they had become "missionized" (Fig. 6.11).

7
PRESERVING
SOUTH TEXAS PREHISTORY

The prehistoric remains in southern Texas are disappearing at an alarming rate. Several factors are responsible for this destruction of the archaeological record. As I have mentioned several times earlier in this book, much of the destruction is due to relic-collecting and untrained digging. This can never be totally stopped, but we should strive to channel the relic-collecting urge toward a more positive goal—that of adding to our growing knowledge of the ancient peoples of the region. This can best be done by participating in the activities of a local, regional, or statewide archaeological society. Local avocational archaeologists and professionals at regional universities and colleges can be contacted. They should be interested in your collections and can show you how to give these collections (and your future collecting activities) greater scientific importance. The professional and the trained avocational archaeologist should strive to work with relic-collectors toward a common goal—preserving the evidence of south Texas prehistory.

After all, it is the relic-collector who is usually on the scene when a site is being destroyed (perhaps by a housing subdivision or other construction activities) and given the proper cooperative atmosphere, the professional or avocational archaeologist can be contacted and information can be saved.

This raises the second factor contributing to the loss of archaeological resources in the region—land modification and construction. As south Texas continues to be developed, the landscape is being drastically changed. Dams are being built, new highways constructed, housing subdivisions are springing up, new sewer lines are going in. All these can lead to the destruction of sites. If the activity is State- or Federally-funded (or licensed) or if the land involved is publicly owned (by a city or county government), then the law requires a professional archaeological survey before any modifications take place. Permits by contractors who seek to initiate construction under these conditions are first reviewed by the Texas Historical Commission in Austin, and if the staff feels that archaeological or historical sites may be endangered, they require an archaeological study.

For example, before the Choke Canyon Dam could be built at Three Rivers in Live Oak County, several years of archaeological work was funded by the U.S. Bureau of Reclamation. When the City of San Antonio planned a sewer line expansion system in 1976, archaeological surveys had to be done of all the proposed lines to make sure that sites would not be damaged. As various uranium-mining companies in Karnes County request permits from the Texas Railroad Commission for pit-mining, archaeological research has to be done first.

The Center for Archaeological Research at The University of Texas at San Antonio, as well as other research units at other state colleges and universities, have done much of this work, often called "contract" or "public" archaeology. The UTSA center carried out more than 200 such studies under these Federal and State guidelines between 1974-1979. The legislation does not seek to hinder development, and it is not the aim of the archaeologists to obstruct construction projects; rather, it is a case of assessing the importance of any archaeological sites in the path of construction. This allows the contractor to plan how to deal with these sites and assures that these irreplaceable resources are not bulldozed aside without proper study. If you have questions about the role of archaeology in Federal- and State-funded projects, or similar projects on publicly owned land, contact the Texas Historical Commission, P. O. Box 12276, Capitol Station, Austin, Texas 78712.

Many construction projects, such as housing subdivisions, are not covered by the legal restrictions noted above; many sites in southern Texas have been destroyed as urban areas continue to expand. Here, we need the help of concerned citizens in reporting the presence of archaeological or historical sites that are endangered by construction. The contractor is usually willing to hold up construction for a brief period while a site is recorded and studied.

Often a developer will see this as a good public relations opportunity. Archaeology can attract "free advertising" for his subdivision when the newspapers and television crews come out to cover an important find.

Sites are also destroyed by the clearing of brush in south Texas pastures. Deep root-plows and heavy chains used to rid a pasture of mesquite and other thorny brush often destroy or heavily damage prehistoric sites. Little can be done about this; the rancher or farmer has the right to improve his property. However, if the local avocational archaeologist or relic-collector can *record* these sites (in the fashion described in Chapter 1), this will be a great deal of help.

In fact, the best way in which we can all work toward preserving the archaeology of southern Texas is through *site recording*. Record information of the sort asked for in Fig. 1.1 and Appendix IV (or write your local archaeological society or university for a supply of site record forms). If you do not want to record a site in a formal way, at least take the time to report its existence by telephoning or writing one of the groups or agencies listed in Appendix I or II. There is a great need for the public to get involved in archaeological preservation, and site recording is the most effective way to make a positive contribution.

Public awareness of archaeology can be created in a variety of ways. If you are an avocational archaeologist, get news releases to your local newspaper on items of archaeological interest. Get your civic clubs to sponsor programs on archaeology. Ask your high school library or your local public library to purchase books which help to explain archaeology. Work with your county historical commission and your local council of governments. (For example, the Coastal Bend Council of Governments, at Corpus Christi, has recently published a very useful public information pamphlet on the archaeology and Indians of that area.) People are curious about their local heritage and the ancient past, and we must cultivate that interest.

If you are interested in archaeology, either as an active collector of Indian artifacts or as one who has read about archaeological excavations in various parts of the world, you ought to seek out persons with similar interests in order to expand your horizons. This is best done by joining an archaeological society. In some parts of the United States, some relic-collecting clubs masquerade as archaeological societies and you should stay away from these if you are really interested in learning. Fortunately, in Texas the local, regional, and state societies are composed of people who want to learn more about archaeology and to apply this knowledge to the study of prehistoric and historic sites. These amateur or avocational archaeologists have made immeasurable contributions to Texas prehistory.

Most of the members started out as either relic-collectors or persons with a vague interest in the ancient past. Through the meetings, programs, and publications of the societies, much valuable training and teaching is accomplished. The key is to participate. Don't worry if the first program you hear seems above your head . . . or if the terminology seems a bit strange.

In 1974, a handful of avocational archaeologists and professional archaeologists got together in San Antonio and formed the Southern Texas Archaeological Association. Its purpose was to appeal to those interested in southern Texas prehistory, be they relic-collectors or Ph.D.'s. It has been a phenomenal success, with its 1979 membership well over 300, and with a quarterly journal which has received national attention. Many of the people who joined had little knowledge of archaeology or perhaps had a box of artifacts they wanted to learn about. Through the programs of the society, many of these people have gone on to do very positive work for the betterment of south Texas archaeology. Other local and regional societies and the state society are listed in Appendix I. Write them or go to one of their meetings. You will find yourself most welcome.

APPENDIX I
ARCHAEOLOGICAL SOCIETIES IN TEXAS

Listed here are most of the archaeological societies in Texas. Membership is open to amateur and professional archaeologists—and the beginner. Those societies which have the most to offer to persons interested in south Texas archaeology are listed first, and descriptions of their activities are provided. The addresses for many of the societies are permanent ones; others may change as officers change within the society. You can usually get the latest address from the office of the Texas Archeological Society. There are some societies not listed here because they were inactive at the time this list was prepared.

Southern Texas Archaeological Association
132 East Crestline
San Antonio, TX 78201

The STAA has more than 300 members. It publishes *La Tierra*, a quarterly journal dealing with south Texas archaeology and the archaeology of adjacent regions. It sponsors quarterly meetings (usually held in San Antonio) and excavation training projects. Dues are $7.50 per year; $15.00 for families.

Texas Archeological Society
Center for Archaeological Research
The University of Texas at San Antonio
San Antonio, TX 78285

The TAS is the statewide society, organized in 1928. It has more than 1,000 members. Annual meetings are held in cities throughout the state. Each June it sponsors a one-week field school (the site for the field school also changes from year to year). The society issues an annual *Bulletin* (250-300 pages) and a quarterly newsletter, *Texas Archeology*. South Texas is often featured in the *Bulletin* and in the newsletter.

Houston Archaeological Society
1706 Oaks Drive
Pasadena, TX 77502
This is also an active society, with monthly meetings held in Houston. Field projects are often carried out. The HAS issues a quarterly *Newsletter*; 63 issues had been published by summer, 1979.

Coastal Bend Archeological Society
c/o 326 Troy
Corpus Christi, TX 78412
It is headquartered in Corpus Christi. Frequent meetings are held, as are occasional field projects.

Webb County Archeological Society
c/o Dr. Leon DeKing
Texas A&I University at Laredo
Laredo, TX 78040
This is a relatively new society, seeking to stimulate interest in scientific archaeology in the Webb County area. Meetings and field trips are held.

Southwest Texas Archaeological Society
c/o 620 Terrell Road
San Antonio, TX 78209
(national AIA address: 53 Park Place, New York, New York 10007)
The society is a chapter of the Archaeological Institute of America and emphasizes Old World archaeology. However, it sponsors lectures which frequently deal with topics on Texas, Mexico, etc.

Other Societies in Texas (listed alphabetically)

Central Texas Archaeological Society, 4229 Mitchell Road, Waco, TX 76710
Concho Valley Archaeological Society, 213 East Ave. D, San Angelo, TX 76901
Dallas Archaeological Society, c/o Archaeology Research Program, Southern Methodist University, Dallas, TX 75275
El Paso Archaeological Society, P. O. Box 4345, El Paso, TX 77914
Iraan Archaeological Society, P. O. Box 183, Iraan, TX 79744
Midland Archaeological Society, P. O. Box 4022, Midland, TX 79701
Panhandle Archaeological Society, P. O. Box 814, Amarillo, TX 79105
Tarrant County Archaeological Society, c/o 413 East Lavender, Arlington, TX 76010
Travis County Archaeological Society, c/o 1507 Lorrain, Austin, TX 78703

APPENDIX II
ACADEMIC PROGRAMS IN SOUTH TEXAS ARCHAEOLOGY

Several universities and colleges in south Texas and adjacent areas have an active involvement or interest in the archaeology of south Texas. Most importantly, they have archaeologists on their faculties or in associated research units who can be of assistance in matters involving south Texas archaeology.

The University of Texas at San Antonio
Center for Archaeological Research
Division of Social Sciences
San Antonio, TX 78285

Anthropology degree program (BA, MA); active research program through the Center; publication series; field schools and contract archaeology projects; archaeology lab; chemical archaeology; phytolith research.

Incarnate Word College
Native American Studies
San Antonio, TX 78284

Anthropology and museum science courses; field school at sites on campus.

San Antonio College
San Antonio, TX 78284

Faculty members teaching anthropology courses.

Trinity University
San Antonio, TX 78284

Anthropology courses.

Texas Southmost College
Department of Behavioral Sciences
Brownsville, TX 78520

Faculty members teaching anthropology courses and involved in local field research.

Pan American University
Edinburg, TX 78539

Faculty members teaching anthropology courses.

Texas A&I University
Kingsville, TX 78363

Faculty members in anthropology, geography, and geology who are involved in local archaeology; local field school; Conner Museum.

Texas A&M University
Department of Sociology and
Anthropology
College Station, TX 77843

Anthropology degree programs;
active research unit doing contract
and grant research; field school;
palynology lab.

The University of Texas at Austin
Texas Archeological Research
Laboratory
Texas Archeological Survey
Radiocarbon Laboratory
Department of Anthropology
Austin, TX 78712

Anthropology degree programs;
active research unit involved in
contract work; archeological laboratory with collections and site records; radiocarbon laboratory.

Rice University
Department of Anthropology
Houston, TX 77001

Anthropology degree programs;
faculty involved in local research.

University of Houston
Department of Anthropology
Houston, TX 77004

Anthropology faculty and degree
program; archaeologist involved
in local field research.

APPENDIX III

ORGANIZATION OF SITE REPORTS

> An excavation without a final, detailed,
> scientific publication must be said to
> mean to science the same as if it had not
> been made.
>
> S. A. Pallis, 1956

This appendix is designed to help the amateur or student to devise a framework through which their site data can be logically arranged. The format can vary, and indeed should vary according to the type of report and the experience gained by the writer. One of the best ways to learn to write is to examine the writings of others; look at site reports published in national, state, or local journals and see how those authors go about presenting archaeological data.

The editor of a journal is usually very willing to help an amateur or student polish up a paper for publication; however, if you use this format, or one similar to it, the job of the editor will be much easier. The format can also be used for reports that are destined for the files of an archaeology laboratory or state agency.

  I. TABLE OF CONTENTS
 II. LIST OF FIGURES AND TABLES
III. ABSTRACT
      Short summary of your report; 1 or 2 paragraphs.
 IV. INTRODUCTION
      What you did and why.
  V. SITE DESCRIPTION
      Describe the site: its location; size; environmental setting; what kind

of work did you do at the site; has work been done there previously?
You might include in this section, or under separate headings, such
topics as "Archaeological Background" (previous work in your
region) or "Ethnohistory" (a summary of historic Indian groups in the
area of your site).

VI. THE ARTIFACTS
Descriptions, typological identifications, measurements; note the
size of your sample; method of study; include provenience tables
showing vertical and horizontal locations—such as unit and level—
of artifacts found.

    A. Chipped Stone
        1. Bifaces
            a. Projectile points (arrow, dart)
            b. Other bifaces (perforators, preforms, gouges, choppers,
               and other tools
        2. Unifaces
            a. Scrapers (various types)
            b. Other unifaces (gravers, trimmed flakes, etc.)
        3. Lithic By-products
            a. cores
            b. flakes (various categories)
            c. appraisal of the technology
    B. Ground Stone
        a. Manos and metates
        b. Hammerstones
        c. Ornaments (pendants, beads, gorgets)
    C. Bone
        a. Implements (awls, flakers, needles)
        b. Ornaments (beads)
    D. Shell
        a. Implements
        b. Ornaments
    E. Ceramics
        a. Sherds
        b. Reconstructed vessels or comments on possible
          vessel shapes
    F. Historic Artifacts (European materials often found in upper
       levels of a prehistoric site: metal, glass, etc.)

VII. SPECIAL STUDIES
    A. Radiocarbon dating
    B. Animal bone analysis
    C. Pollen or phytolith studies
    D. Midden constituent analysis
    E. Shell analyses (snails; marine shells)
    F. Soil chemistry

VIII. DISCUSSION AND INTERPRETATION
Review what you have done; how can the site be interpreted; com-

pare with nearby sites; how does the site fit into the regional chronological framework; what can you say about the function of the site
and the activities of its ancient peoples? What could be done in the
future at the site to get better data?

IX. SUMMARY

Summarize your report for the reader; relate the major findings,
interpretations, and conclusions.

X. ACKNOWLEDGMENTS

Thank your crew, your colleagues, the landowner, the typist, etc.

XI. REFERENCES CITED

In this section—the bibliography—list only those publications directly cited in the text; consult local or state journals for format, as it will
vary. In general, list by author (alphabetically), being certain to include the *full* title of an article and the journal in which it was published, and the pagination; for books, list the title, publisher, and city
of publication.

In preparing illustrations for your report, be sure to make all line
drawings in black ink. Line drawings or photographic illustrations
are called "Figures"; be sure they are cited in the text and prepare a
descriptive caption for each.

All lists of tabulated information are called "Tables"; they must
also be titled and cited in the text. Maps should be carefully drawn
(in most journals they are referred to as "Figures", not as "Maps").
Do not hand-letter them unless you are particularly skilled at this.
The various brands of press-on lettering are an invaluable aid in
preparing nice illustrations.

APPENDIX IV
SAMPLE
RECORD FORMS

LEVEL RECORD FORM   Site No._____

                          Site Name _____

Unit _____ Level _____ Date _____

Excavators: _____ Screen Size _____

Description of level/midden (color, composition, contents, etc.) _____

_____

_____

_____

_____

_____

Materials recovered: (a) chipped stone _____

_____

(b) animal bone _____

(c) shell (mussel, land snails) _____

(d) ceramics, metal, glass, etc. _____

Artifacts (briefly describe and draw; use reverse if necessary):

Features _____ (Use separate form for recording features)

Disturbances _____

Photographs_____ No. of bags _____

Recorded by_____

ARCHAEOLOGICAL PHOTOGRAPHIC RECORD

Site_____ Photographer_____

Camera_____ Film_____

NEG CAT #	DATE	ROLL - PACK	SHOT #	SUBJECT (Indicate Direction; Note Scale)

SPECIMEN CATALOG

Permanent Site No._____

Temporary Site No.

or Name _____

Date _____

Lot No.	No. of Specimens	Description	Location		Remarks
			Horizontal	Vertical	

FEATURE REPORT   Permanent Site No._____

Temporary Site No.

or Name _____

Date _____

Unit_____Level_____

Horizontal Location_____

Vertical Location (from surface or from datum)_____

_____

Description of feature_____

_____

_____

_____

Dimensions_____ Associations_____

_____

Field interpretation of feature_____

_____

Drawing of feature (use reverse; indicate North; give scale used).
Sketch or description of associated artifacts/materials:

Photographs_____

Disposal of feature/associated artifacts_____

_____

Recorded by_____

BURIAL RECORD Permanent Site No._____

Temporary Site No.

or Name _____

Subject _____

Horizontal location _____

Skull elev. _____From surface _____

Pelvis elev. _____From surface _____

Stratigraphic relationships _____

Evidence of being intrusive _____

Grave fill _____

Fill into which grave was dug _____

Grave dimensions _____

Type of burial _____Preservation _____

Position of skeleton_____

Orientation _____Direction of skull _____Facing _____

Posthumous shifting of bones _____

Bones absent (or present) _____

Age _____ Sex _____ Pathology _____

Associated objects (itemize) _____

_____

_____

Remarks _____

_____

_____

_____

Disposal of specimens _____

_____

Cat. nos. _____

Drawing/Sketch:

Photos _____

Recorded by _____ Date _____

APPENDIX V
JOURNALS AND
MONOGRAPHS

If you wish to pursue the study of south Texas archaeology, there are several journals to which you can subscribe. I have also listed journals of broader scope which would allow the amateur and student to keep abreast of other developments in archaeology and further expand their knowledge of methods and techniques.

JOURNALS

La Tierra, Journal of the Southern Texas Archaeological Association (quarterly)

Bulletin of the Texas Archeological Society (annual)

Texas Archeology, Newsletter of the Texas Archeological Society (the *Bulletin* and the newsletter come with your membership in the TAS)

The Artifact, Journal of the El Paso Archaeological Society (quarterly)

Texas Journal of Science, Texas Academy of Science, c/o Angelo State University, San Angelo (quarterly)

The Record, Newsletter of the Dallas Archaeological Society (occasional)

Newsletter, Houston Archaeological Society (quarterly)

Plains Anthropologist, Journal of the Plains Conference, 410 Wedgewood Drive, Lincoln, NE 68510 (quarterly)

NATIONAL AND INTERNATIONAL JOURNALS

American Antiquity, Society for American Archaeology, 1703 New Hampshire Ave., NW, Washington, D.C. 20009 (quarterly)

American Anthropologist, American Anthropological Association, 1703 New Hampshire Ave., NW, Washington, D.C. 20009 (bimonthly)

Archaeology, Archaeological Institute of America, 53 Park Place, New York, NY 10007 (bimonthly)

Historical Archaeology, Society for Historical Archaeology, 1703 New Hampshire Ave., NW, Washington, D.C. 20009 (annual)

Journal of Field Archaeology, Association for Field Archaeology, Boston University Scholarly Publications, 25 Buick St., Boston, MA 02215 (quarterly)

Journal of New World Archaeology, Institute of Archaeology, University of California at Los Angeles, Los Angeles, CA 90024 (irregular but frequent)

North American Archeologist, Baywood Publishing Co., Inc., 120 Marine St., P. O. Box 609, Farmingdale, NY 11735 (quarterly)

Popular Archaeology, P. O. Box 4211, Arlington, VA 22204 (bimonthly)

World Archaeology, Routledge & Kegan Paul Ltd., Newtown Road, Henley-on-Thames, Oxon RG9 1EN England (quarterly)

MONOGRAPH SERIES

The following agencies and institutions in Texas publish reports and monographs, some of them dealing with south Texas and related areas. Write them for a current list of available publications.

Center for Archaeological Research, The University of Texas at San Antonio, San Antonio, TX 78285: *Archaeological Survey Reports, Special Reports, Guidebooks in Archaeology,* and other series.

Texas Historical Commission, Office of the State Archeologist, P. O. Box 12276, Austin, TX 78712: various series.

Texas A&M University, Department of Sociology and Anthropology, College Station, TX 77843: *Anthropology Laboratory Reports* and other publications.

State Department of Highways and Public Transportation, Archaeology Section, Highway Design Division, Austin, TX 78701: *Publications in Archaeology.*

Texas Archeological Survey and Texas Archeological Research Laboratory, Balcones Research Center, 10,000 Burnet Road, Austin, TX 78758: *Papers, Research Reports,* and other publications.

Department of Anthropology, The University of Texas at Austin, Austin, TX 78712: *Anthropology Series;* none issued since 1969.

Texas Memorial Museum, The University of Texas at Austin, Austin, TX 78712: *Bulletin, Pearce-Sellards Series,* and other publications.

Southern Methodist University, Department of Anthropology, Archaeology Research Program, Dallas, TX 75275: *Research Reports; SMU Contributions in Anthropology.*

Occasional publications issued by Texas Tech Museum; and Department of Anthropology, Texas Tech University, Lubbock, TX 79409.

REFERENCES CITED

Allen, D., and E. P. Cheatum
    1960 Ecological Implications of Fresh Water and Land Gastropods in Texas Archeological Sites. *Bulletin of the Texas Archeological Society,* Vol. 31: 291-316.

Almaraz, F. D., Jr.
    1979 Crossroad of Empire: The Church and State on the Rio Grande Frontier of Coahuila and Texas, 1700-1821. *Archaeology and History of the San Juan Bautista Mission Area, Coahuila and Texas, Report 1.* Center for Archaeological Research. The University of Texas at San Antonio.

Berlandier, J. L.
    1969 *The Indians of Texas in 1830.* Edited and annotated by John C. Ewers. Smithsonian Institution, Washington, D.C.

Birmingham, W. W., and T. R. Hester
    1976 Late Pleistocene Archaeological Remains from the Johnston-Heller Site, Texas Coastal Plain. *Center for Archaeological Research, The University of Texas at San Antonio, Special Report,* No. 3: 15-33.

Blair, W. F.
    1950 The Biotic Provinces of Texas. *Texas Journal of Science,* Vol. 1, No. 2: 93-116.

Calhoun, C. A.
    1964 A Polychrome Vessel from the Texas Coastal Bend. *Bulletin of the Texas Archeological Society,* Vol. 35: 205-212

Campbell, T. N.
    1947 The Johnson Site: Type Site of the Aransas Focus of the Texas Coast. *Bulletin of the Texas Archeological and Paleontological Society,* Vol. 18: 40-75.

1952 The Kent-Crane Site: A Shell Midden on the Texas Coast. *Bulletin of the Texas Archeological Society*, Vol. 23: 39-77.

1961 Origins of Pottery Types from the Coastal Bend Region of Texas. *Bulletin of the Texas Archeological Society*, Vol. 32: 331-336.

1975 The Payaya Indians of Southern Texas. *Southern Texas Archaeological Association, Special Publication No. 1*, San Antonio.

1977 Ethnic Identities of Extinct Coahuiltecan Populations: Case of the Juanca Indians. *The Pearce-Sellards Series*, No. 26. Texas Memorial Museum, Austin.

1979 Ethnohistoric Notes on Indian Groups Associated with Three Spanish Missions at Guerrero, Coahuila. *Archaeology and History of the San Juan Bautista Mission Area, Coahuila and Texas, Report No. 3*. Center for Archaeological Research, The University of Texas at San Antonio.

Campbell, T. N., and T. R. Hester
MS Ethnohistorical and Archaeological Notes on the Pacuache Indians of Southern Texas. Manuscript to be submitted for publication.

Chadderdon, M. F.
1976 An Analysis of Altered Quartzite Cobbles from Victoria County, Texas. *La Tierra*, Vol. 3, No. 1: 6-15.

Collins, M. B., and T. R. Hester
1968 A Wooden Mortar and Pestle from Val Verde County, Texas. *Bulletin of the Texas Archeological Society*, Vol. 39: 1-8.

Collins, M. B., T. R. Hester, and F. A. Weir
1969 The Floyd Morris Site (41 CF 2): A Prehistoric Cemetery Site in Cameron County, Texas. *Bulletin of the Texas Archeological Society*, Vol. 40: 119-146.

Corbin, J. E.
1963 Archeological Materials from the Northern Shore of Corpus Christi Bay, Texas. *Bulletin of the Texas Archeological Society*, Vol. 34: 5-30.

1974 A Model for Cultural Succession for the Coastal Bend Area of Texas. *Bulletin of the Texas Archeological Society*, Vol. 45: 29-54.

Covey, C. (editor)
1972 *Cabeza de Vaca's Adventures in the Unknown Interior of America*. Collier Books, New York.

Dibble, D. S., and D. Lorrain
1967 Bonfire Shelter: A Stratified Bison Kill Site, Val Verde County, Texas. *Texas Memorial Museum, Miscellaneous Papers*, No. 1.

Dillehay, T. D.
1974 Late Quaternary Bison Population Changes on the Southern Plains. *Plains Anthropologist*, Vol. 19, No. 65: 180-196.

Duffield, L. F.
1970 Vertisols and Their Implications for Archeological Research. *American Anthropologist*, 72(5): 1055-1062.

Epstein, J. F.
1969 The San Isidro Site, An Early Man Campsite in Nuevo Leon, Mexico. *Anthropology Series*, No. 7. Department of Anthropology, The University of Texas at Austin.

Fehrenbach, T. R.
1974 *Comanches. The Destruction of a People*. Alfred A. Knopf, New York.

Fenley, F.
1957 *Oldtimers of Southwest Texas*. Hornby Press, Uvalde, Texas.

Fitzpatrick, W. S., J. Fitzpatrick, and T. N. Campbell
1964 A Rockport Black-on-Gray Vessel from the Vicinity of Corpus Christi, Texas. *Bulletin of the Texas Archeological Society*, Vol. 35: 193-204.

Fox, A. A., and W. S. Fitzpatrick
1977 A Polychrome Vessel from Goliad County, Southern Texas. *Bulletin of the Texas Archeological Society*, Vol. 48: 133-138.

Fox, D. E.
1979 The Lithic Artifacts of Indians at the Spanish Colonial Missions, San Antonio, Texas. *Center for Archaeological Research, The University of Texas at San Antonio, Special Report*, No. 8.

Fox, D. E., R. J. Mallouf, N. O'Malley, and W. M. Sorrow
1974 Archeological Resources of the Proposed Cuero I Reservoir, DeWitt and Gonzales Counties, Texas. *Texas Historical Commission and Texas Water Development Board, Archeological Survey Report*, No. 12. Austin.

Gatschet, A. S.
1891 The Karankawa Indians, the Coast People of Texas. *Archaeological and Ethnological Papers of the Peabody Museum*, Vol. 1, No. 2.

Gerstle, A., T. C. Kelly, and C. Assad
1978 The Fort Sam Houston Project: An Archaeological and Historical Assessment. *Center for Archaeological Research, The University of Texas at San Antonio, Archaeological Survey Report*, No. 40.

Gibson, A. M.
1963 *The Kickapoos: Lords of the Middle Border*. University of Oklahoma Press, Norman.

Goggin, J. M.
  1951 The Mexican Kickapoo Indians. *Southwestern Journal of Anthropology,* Vol. 7:314-327.
Harris, D. R.
  1966 Recent Plant Invasions in the Arid and Semiarid Southwest of the United States. *Annals, American Association of Geographers,* Vol. 56: 408-422.
Hester, T. R.
  1968 Paleo-Indian Artifacts from Sites Along San Miguel Creek: Frio, Atascosa and McMullen Counties, Texas. *Bulletin of the Texas Archeological Society,* Vol. 39: 147-162.
  1969a Archeological Investigations in Kenedy and Kleberg Counties, Texas, August, 1967. *State Building Commission, Archeological Program, Report,* No. 15. Austin.
  1969b The Floyd Morris and Ayala Sites: A Discussion of Burial Practices in the Rio Grande Valley and the Lower Texas Coast. *Bulletin of the Texas Archeological Society,* Vol. 40: 147-166.
  1969c Human Bone Artifacts from Southern Texas. *American Antiquity,* Vol. 34, No. 3: 326-328.
  1970 Burned Rock Middens on the Southwestern Edge of the Edwards Plateau, Texas. *Plains Anthropologist,* Vol. 15, No. 50: 237-250.
  1971a Archeological Investigations at the La Jita Site, Uvalde County, Texas. *Bulletin of the Texas Archeological Society,* Vol. 42: 51-148.
  1971b Hafted Unifaces from Southwestern Coahuila. *The Kiva,* Vol. 36, No. 4: 36-41.
  1971c An "Eolith" from Lower Pleistocene Deposits of Southern Texas. *Bulletin of the Texas Archeological Society,* Vol. 42: 367-342.
  1972 Toltec Artifacts from Southern Texas. *Southwest Museum Masterkey,* Vol. 46, No. 4: 137-140.
  1975 Chipped Stone Industries on the Rio Grande Plain, Texas: Some Preliminary Observations. *Texas Journal of Science,* Vol. 26, Nos. 1-2; 213-222.
  1977a A Painted Pebble from a Site on the Nueces River, Southern Texas. *Bulletin of the Texas Archeological Society,* Vol. 48: 139-144.
  1977b The Lithic Technology of Mission Indians in Texas and Northeastern Mexico. *Lithic Technology,* Vol. 6, Nos. 1-2: 9-13.
  1977c Archaeological Research at the Hinojosa Site (41 JW 8), Jim Wells County, Southern Texas. *Center for Archaeological Research, The University of Texas at San Antonio, Archaeological Survey Report,* No. 42.
  1978 Background to the Archaeology of Chaparrosa Ranch, Southern Texas. *Center for Archaeological Research, The University of Texas at San Antonio, Special Report,* No. 6, Vol. 1.
  1979 Early Populations in Prehistoric Texas. *Archaeology,* Vol. 32, No. 6: 26-33.
  1980 Tradition and Diversity Among the Prehistoric Hunters and

Gatherers of Southern Texas. *Plains Anthropologist* (in press, for 1981).

Hester, T. R., and J. C. Corbin
1975 Two Burial Sites on the Central Texas Coast. *Texas Journal of Science*, Vol. 26, Nos. 1-2: 286-289.

Hester, T. R., D. Gilbow, and A. Albee
1973 A Functional Analysis of Clear Fork Artifacts from the Rio Grande Plain of Texas. *American Antiquity*, Vol. 38, No. 1: 90-96.

Hester, T. R., R. F. Heizer, and J. A. Graham
1975 *Field Methods in Archaeology*. 6th edition. Mayfield Publishing Company, Palo Alto, California.

Hester, T. R., and T. C. Hill, Jr.
1971a An Initial Study of a Prehistoric Ceramic Tradition in Southern Texas. *Plains Anthropologist*, Vol. 16, No. 52: 195-203.
1971b Notes on Scottsbluff Points from the Texas Coastal Plain. *Southwestern Lore*, Vol. 37, No. 1: 27-33.
1973 Prehistoric Occupation at the Holdsworth and Stewart Sites on the Rio Grande Plain of Texas. *Bulletin of the Texas Archeological Society*, Vol. 43: 33-75.
1975 Some Aspects of Late Prehistoric and Protohistoric Archaeology in Southern Texas. *Center for Archaeological Research, The University of Texas at San Antonio, Special Report*, No. 1.

Hester, T. R., and R. Parker
1970 The Berclair Site: A Late Prehistoric Component in Goliad County, Southern Texas. *Bulletin of the Texas Archeological Society*, Vol. 41: 1-24.

Hester, T. R., and R. Rodgers
1971 Additional Data on the Burial Practices of the Brownsville Complex, Southern Texas. *Texas Journal of Science*, Vol. 22, No. 4: 367-371.

Hester, T. R., and H. J. Shafer
1975 An Initial Study of Blade Technology on the Central and Southern Texas Coast. *Plains Anthropologist*, Vol. 20, No. 69: 175-185.

Hester, T. R., L. D. White, and J. White
1969 Archeological Materials from the Oulline Site and Other Sites in LaSalle County, Texas. *Texas Journal of Science*, Vol. 21, No. 2: 130-165.

Highley, L., C. Graves, C. Land, and G. Judson
1978 Archeological Investigations at Scorpion Cave (41 ME 7), Medina County, Texas. *Bulletin of the Texas Archeological Society*, Vol. 49: 139-198.

Hill, T. C., Jr.
    1975 Experiments in Pottery-Making. *La Tierra*, Vol. 2, No. 3: 4-30.

Hill, T. C., Jr., and T. R. Hester
    1971 Isolated Late Prehistoric and Archaic Components at the Honey-moon Site (41 ZV 34), Southern Texas. *Plains Anthropologist*, Vol. 15, No. 51: 52-59.
    1973 A Preliminary Report on the Tortuga Flat Site: A Protohistoric Campsite in Southern Texas. *Texas Archeology*, Vol. 17, No. 2: 10-14.

Hill, T. C., Jr., J. B. Holdsworth, and T. R. Hester
    1972 Yucca Exploitation: A Contemporary Account from the Rio Grande Plain. In *Archaeological Papers Presented to J. W. House* (T. R. Hester, ed.): 10-11. Berkeley.

Inglis, J. M.
    1964 A History of Vegetation on the Rio Grande Plain. *Texas Parks and Wildlife Bulletin*, No. 45. Austin.

Johnson, L., Jr.
    1964 The Devil's Mouth Site, A Stratified Campsite at Amistad Reservoir. *Archaeology Series, No. 6*. Department of Anthropology, The University of Texas at Austin.

Johnson, L., Jr., D. A. Suhm, and C. D. Tunnell
    1962 Salvage Archeology of Canyon Reservoir: The Wunderlich, Footbridge and Oblate Sites. *Texas Memorial Museum, Bulletin*, No. 5.

Kelley, D.
    1971 The Tonkawas. In: *Indian Tribes of Texas*, pp. 151-168. Texian Press, Waco.

Kirkland, F., and W. W. Newcomb, Jr.
    1967 *The Rock Art of Texas Indians*. University of Texas Press, Austin.

Kroeber, A. L.
    1925 Handbook of the California Indians. *Bulletin, Bureau of American Ethnology*, No. 78.

LaTorre, F. A., and D. L.
    1976 *The Mexican Kickapoo Indians*. University of Texas Press, Austin.

Lynn, W. M., D. E. Fox, and N. O'Malley
    1977 Cultural Resource Survey of Choke Canyon Reservoir, Live Oak and McMullen Counties, Texas. *Office of the State Archeologist, Texas Historical Commission, Archeological Survey Report*, No. 20.

MacNeish, R. S.
    1958 Preliminary Archaeological Investigations in the Sierra de Tamau-

lipas, Mexico. *Transactions, American Philosophical Society,* Vol. 48, Part 6.

Mallouf, R. J., B. J. Baskin, and K. L. Killen
1977 A Predictive Assessment of Cultural Resources in Hidalgo and Willacy Counties, Texas. *Texas Historical Commission, Office of the State Archeologist, Survey Report,* No. 25. Austin.

Montgomery, J. L.
1978 The Mariposa Site: A Late Prehistoric Site on the Rio Grande Plain of Texas. *Center for Archaeological Research, The University of Texas at San Antonio, Special Report,* No. 6, Vol. 2.

Myres, S.L.
1971 The Lipan Apaches. In: *Indian Tribes of Texas,* pp. 129-145. Texian Press, Waco.

Newcomb, W. W., Jr.
1961 *The Indians of Texas, from Prehistoric to Modern Times.* University of Texas Press, Austin. (Also in a later paperback edition.)

Pitzer, J. M.
1977 A Guide to the Identification of Burins in Prehistoric Chipped Stone Assemblages. *Center for Archaeological Research, The University of Texas at San Antonio, Guidebooks in Archaeology,* No. 1.

Prewitt, E. R.
1974 Preliminary Archeological Investigations in the Rio Grande Delta of Texas. *Bulletin of the Texas Archeological Society,* Vol. 45: 55-66.

Robinson, R. L.
1979 The Study of Biosilica: Reconstructing the Paleoenvironment of the Central Coastal Plain of Texas. *Center for Archaeological Research, The University of Texas at San Antonio, Special Report 7.*

Ruecking, F. A., Jr.
1954 Ceremonies of the Coahuiltecan Indians of Southern Texas and Northeastern Mexico. *Texas Journal of Science,* Vol. 7, No. 3: 330-339.
1955 The Coahuiltecan Indians of Southern Texas and Northeastern Mexico. Unpublished MA thesis, on file at The University of Texas at Austin.

Ruiz, J. F.
1972 *Report on the Indian Tribes of Texas in 1828.* Translation edited and annotated by John C. Ewers. Yale University Library, New Haven.

Schuetz, M. K.
1969 The History and Archaeology of Mission San Juan Capistrano,

San Antonio, Texas. Volume II. *State Building Commission, Archeological Program, Report*, No. 11.

Sellards, E. H.
1940 Pleistocene Artifacts and Associated Fossils from Bee County, Texas. *Bulletin of the Geological Society of America*, Vol. 51: 1627-1657.

Shafer, H. J.
1969 Archeological Investigations in the Robert Lee Reservoir, West Central Texas. *Texas Archeological Salvage Project*, Papers, No. 17.

Shafer, H. J., and E. P. Baxter
1975 An Archeological Survey of the Lignite Project, Atascosa and McMullen Counties, Texas. *Anthropology Laboratory, Report No. 7*. Texas A&M University.

Shafer, H. J., and T. R. Hester
1971 A Study of the Function and Technology of Certain Bifacial Tools from Southern Texas. *Texas Historical Survey Committee, Archeological Report*, No. 20.

Shantz, H. L.
1924 *Atlas of American Agriculture. The Physical Basis of Agriculture. Natural Vegetation. Grassland and Desert Shrubs*. Government Printing Office, Washington, D.C.

Sjoberg, A. F.
1953a The Culture of the Tonkawa, A Texas Indian Tribe. *Texas Journal of Science*, Vol. 5: 280-304.
1953b Lipan Apache Culture in Historical Perspective. *Southwestern Journal of Anthropology*, Vol. 9: 76-98.

Suhm, D. A., and E. B. Jelks
1962 Handbook of Texas Archeology: Type Descriptions. *Texas Archeological Society, Special Publication*, No. 1, and *Texas Memorial Museum, Bulletin*, No. 4. Austin.

Suhm, D. A., A. D. Krieger, and E. B. Jelks
1954 An Introductory Handbook of Texas Archeology. *Bulletin of the Texas Archeological Society*, Vol. 25.

Tunnell, C. D., and W. W. Newcomb, Jr.
1969 A Lipan Apache Mission, San Lorenzo de la Santa Cruz, 1762-1771. *Texas Memorial Museum Bulletin*, No. 14. Austin.

Wallace, E., and E. A. Hoebel
1952 *The Comanches: Lords of the South Plains*. University of Oklahoma Press, Norman.

Weir, F. A.
1956 Surface Artifacts from La Perdida, Starr County, Texas. *Bulletin of*

the *Texas Archeological Society*, Vol. 26: 59-78.

Word, J. H., and C. L. Douglas
    1970 Excavations at Baker Cave, Val Verde County, Texas. *Texas Memorial Museum*, Bulletin, No. 16.

Word, J. H., and A. Fox
    1975 The Cogdell Burial in Floyd County, Texas. *Bulletin of the Texas Archeological Society*, Vol. 46: 1-64.

FURTHER READING

In addition to those references cited directly in the text, the reader may wish to consult some of the items listed here as suggestions for further reading.

Chapter 1

Following is a sample of some of the many books that provide an introduction to archaeology, archaeological methods, and archaeological findings. Some of these are college-level texts and will have to be ordered through your local bookstore.

Bordes, F.
    1968 *The Old Stone Age*. World University Library, McGraw-Hill, New York.

Brennan, L. A.
    1973 *Beginner's Guide to Archaeology*. Dell, New York.

Ceram, C. W.
    1958 *The March of Archaeology*. A. Knopf, New York.
    1972 *Gods, Graves and Scholars*. Bantam Books, New York.

Chang, K. C.
    1967 *Rethinking Archaeology*. Random House, New York.

Clark, G.
    1977 *World Prehistory in New Perspective*. Cambridge University Press, New York.

Coles, J. M., and E. S. Higgs
    1975 *The Archaeology of Early Man*. Peregrine, Penguin Books, Baltimore.

Daniel, G.
   1967 *The Origins and Growth of Archaeology.* Pelican A885, Penguin Books, Baltimore.
   1968 *Man Discovers His Past.* T. Y. Crowell, New York.

Deetz, J.
   1967 *Invitation to Archaeology.* Natural History Press, Garden City, New York.

Fagan, B. M.
   1977 *People of the Earth.* Little, Brown and Company, Boston.
   1978 *In the Beginning.* Little, Brown and Company, Boston.

Heizer, R. F.
   1962 *Man's Discovery of his Past.* Prentice-Hall (See more recent paper edition; Peek Publications, Palo Alto, California.)

Hester, T. R., R. F. Heizer, and J. A. Graham
   1975 *Field Methods in Archaeology.* 6th ed. Mayfield Publishing Company, Palo Alto, California.

Hester, T. R., R. F. Heizer, and C. Graves
   1980 *Bibliography of Archaeology: A Guide to Basic Archaeological Literature.* Garland, New York.

Hole, F., and R. F. Heizer
   1973 *Introduction to Prehistoric Archaeology.* Holt, Rinehart, and Winston, New York.

MacNeish, R. S.
   1973 *Early Man in America: Readings from Scientific American.* W. H. Freeman, San Francisco.

Robbins, M.
   1965 *Amateur Archaeologist's Handbook.* T. Y. Crowell, New York.

Smith, J. W.
   1976 *Foundations of Archaeology.* Glencoe Press, Beverly Hills.

Thomas, D. H.
   1979 *Archaeology.* Holt, Rinehart and Winston, New York.

Wheeler, M.
   1964 *Archaeology from the Earth.* Pelican, Penguin Books, Baltimore.

Willey, G. R., and J. Sabloff
   1974 *A History of American Archaeology.* W. H. Freeman, San Francisco.

Wilson, D.
   1974 *The New Archaeology.* New American Library, New York.

Wooley, L.
   1963 *Digging Up the Past.* Pelican, Penguin Books, Baltimore.

Chapter 2

Development of North American Prehistoric Cultures:

Adams, R. E. W.
1977 *Prehistoric Mesoamerica*. Little Brown and Company, Boston.

Jennings, J. D.
1974 *Prehistory of North America*. McGraw-Hill, New York.

Jennings, J. D., and E. Norbeck, editors
1964 *Prehistoric Man in the New World*. University of Chicago Press.

Willey, G. R.
1966 *An Introduction to American Archaeology*, Vol. 1: *North and Middle America*. Prentice-Hall, Inc., Englewood Cliffs, New Jersey.

South Texas environment:

Bogush, E. R.
1952 Brush Invasion in the Rio Grande Plain of Texas. *Texas Journal of Science*, Vol. 4, No. 1: 85-91.

Brune, G.
1975 *Major and Historical Springs of Texas*. Texas Water Development Board, Report 189. Austin.

Bryant, V. M., Jr., and H. J. Shafer
1977 The Late Quaternary Paleoenvironment of Texas: A Model for the Archeologist. *Bulletin of the Texas Archeological Society*, Vol. 48: 1-26.

Carr, J. T.
1967 *The Climate and Physiography of Texas*. Texas Water Development Board, Report 53. Austin.

Cook, O. F.
1908 Change of Vegetation on the South Texas Prairies. *United States Department of Agriculture, Bureau of Plant Industry, Circular No. 14*. Washington, D.C.

Fenneman, N. M.
1931 *Physiography of Eastern United States*. McGraw-Hill, New York.

Geology and Ground Water Resources:

Various volumes on several south Texas counties, Bulletins issued by the Texas Board of Water Engineers, Austin.

Gould, F. W.
1969 *Texas Plants: A Checklist and Ecological Summary*. Texas A&M University, MP-585, Revised. College Station, Texas.

Havard, V.
1884 The Mezquit. *American Naturalist*, Vol. 18: 451-459.
1885 Report on the Flora of Western and Southern Texas. *Proceedings, United States National Museum*, Volume 8: 445-533. Washington, D.C.

Hester, T. R.
1976 *Hunters and Gatherers of the Rio Grande Plain and the Lower Coast of Texas*. Center for Archaeological Research, The University of Texas at San Antonio.

Johnston, M. C.
1963 Past and Present Grasslands of Southern Texas and Northeastern Mexico. *Ecology*, Vol. 44, No. 3: 456-466.

Kroeber, A. L.
1939 Cultural and Natural Areas of Native North America. *University of California Publications in American Archaeology and Ethnology*, Vol. 38.

Pool, W. C.
1975 *A Historical Atlas of Texas*. Encino Press, Austin.

Price, W. A.
1958 Sedimentology and Quaternary Geomorphology of South Texas. *Gulf Coast Association of Geological Societies, Corpus Christi Geological Society, Field Trip Manual*: 41-75.

Price, W. A., and G. Gunter
1943 Certain Recent Geological and Biological Changes in South Texas, with Consideration of Probable Causes. *Proceedings and Transactions of the Texas Academy of Science—1942*: 3-21.

Russell, R. J.
1945 Climates of Texas. *Annals, American Association of Geographers*, Vol. 35: 37-52.

Sheldon, R. A.
1979 *Roadside Geology of Texas*. Mountain Press, Missoula, Montana.

Soil Surveys of Texas Counties:

Available for many south Texas counties; prepared by the United States Department of Agriculture, Soil Conservation Service.

Trowbridge, A. C.
1922 A Geologic Reconnaissance in the Gulf Coastal Plain of Texas, Near the Rio Grande. *Shorter Contributions to General Geology, Professional Paper*, No. 131. U. S. Geological Survey, Washington, D.C.

Wells, P. V.
> 1970 Postglacial Vegetational History of the Great Plains. *Science*, Vol. 167: 1574-1582.

Wynd, F. L.
> 1944 The Geologic and Physiographic Background of the Soils in the Lower Rio Grande Valley of Texas. *American Midland Naturalist*, Vol. 32, No. 1: 200-235.

Chapter 3

Driver, H. E., and W. C. Massey
> 1957 *Comparative Studies of North American Indians*. Transactions, American Philosophical Society, Vol. 47, Part 2. Philadelphia.

Ewers, J. C.
> 1973 The Influence of Epidemics on the Indian Populations and Cultures of Texas. *Plains Anthropologist*, Vol. 18, No. 60: 104-115.

Faulk, O. B.
> 1969 The Comanche Invasion of Texas, 1743-1836. *Great Plains Journal*, Vol. 9, No. 1: 10-50.

Gatschet, A. S.
> *The Karankawa Indians, The Coast People of Texas*. Archaeological and Ethnological Papers of the Peabody Museum, Vol. I, No. 2. 1891.

Jones, W. K.
> 1969 *Notes on the History and Material Culture of the Tonkawa Indians*. Smithsonian Contributions to Anthropology, Vol. 2, No. 5, Washington.

Ruecking, F. A., Jr.
> 1953 The Economic System of the Coahuiltecan Indians of Southern Texas and Northeastern Mexico. *Texas Journal of Science*, Vol. 6, No. 3, 480-497.
> 1955 The Social Organization of the Coahuiltecan Indians of Southern Texas and Northeastern Mexico. *Texas Journal of Science*, Vol. 7, No. 4, 357-388.

Skeels, L. L. M.
> 1972 An Ethnohistorical Survey of Texas Indians. *Texas Historical Survey Committee, Office of the State Archeologist, Report No. 22.* Austin.

Vigness, D. M.
> 1955 Indian Raids on the Lower Rio Grande, 1836-1837. *Southwestern Historical Quarterly*, Vol. 55, No. 1: 14-23.

Winfrey, D. H. and others
    1971 *Indian Tribes of Texas*. Texian Press, Waco.

Chapter 4

Bulletin of the Texas Archeological Society
    Various issues contain reports on sites in south, south central, and southwestern Texas. See especially Vols. 34, 38, 39, 40, 45, and 49.

La Tierra, Journal of the Southern Texas Archaeological Association
    Most issues of this quarterly contain descriptions of different kinds of sites in the south Texas region.

Chapter 5

The following readings can provide more information on stone tool-making and stone tool use. Some are also of benefit to those interested in experimenting with flint-chipping.

Bordaz, J.
    1970 *Tools of the Old and New Stone Age*. Natural History Press, Garden City, New York.

Bordes, F.
    1968 *The Old Stone Age*. World University Library, McGraw-Hill, New York.

Crabtree, D. E.
    1972 An Introduction to Flintworking. *Occasional Papers, Idaho State University Museum*, No. 28. (Available through University Bookstore, Pocatello, Idaho.)

Mewhinney, H.
    1957 *A Manual for Neanderthals*. The University of Texas Press, Austin (3rd printing, 1972).

Morris, J. M.
    1973 *Flint Flaking*. Privately published, Kerrville, Texas. (Available from author, at Box 755, Kerrville, Texas 78208.)

Oakley, K. P.
    1959 *Man the Tool-Maker*. Phoenix Books, P-20. University of Chicago Press.

Semenov, S. A.
    1964 *Prehistoric Technology: an experimental study of the oldest tools and artifacts from traces of manufacture and wear*. Translated by M. W. Thompson. Barnes and Noble, New York.

Swanson, E., editor
>1975 *Lithic Technology: Making and Using Stone Tools.* Aldine, Chicago.

Chapter 6

Jelks, E. B., et al., editors
>1958 A Review of Texas Archeology: Part One. *Bulletin of the Texas Archeological Society,* Vol. 29.

Sayles, E. B.
>1935 *An Archaeological Survey of Texas.* Medallion Papers, No. 17. Gila Pueblo, Arizona.

Suhm, D. A., E. B. Jelks, and A. D. Krieger
>1954 An Introductory Handbook of Texas Archeology. *Bulletin of the Texas Archeological Society,* Vol. 25.

INDEX

Page numbers in **boldface type** indicate illustrations.

Alamo, 164
Alibates flint, 130
animals, prehistoric, 36-37, 132, **137**, 141, 149-150, 158-160
Aransas County, sites in, 154
Aransas Phase, 122
archaeology
  contract, 8, 166
  definitions of, 2, 3
  degrees in, 171-172
  field methods, 11-23
  goals of, 3
  journals, 181-182
  societies, 169-170
Archaic period
  North America, 29-30
  Texas, 149-154
arrow points, 94, 105-108, 158
  types of, **104**, 105-108, **107**, **123**, 145
artifacts,
  definition of, 7
  types of, 87-130
    bifaces, 87
    exotic, 128, **129**, 130
    bone and antler, **70**, **80**, **116**, 120, **121**
    chipped stone, 87-114
    flakes, 90, **91**
    ground stone, 115, **116**, **117**, **118**, **119**, 120
    human bone, **76**
    painted pebbles, 87, **88**
    pottery, **121**, 122, 124, **125**, 126, 128, 154

projectile points, 94-108 (**97**, **99**, **100**, **103**, **104**, **107**)
  shell, 120, 122, **123**
asphaltum, 50, 102, 112, 125, 128
Atascosa County, sites in, 94, 154
atlatl (see spearthrower)
auxiliary sites, 64-66
Ayala site, 7, **74**

Baffin Bay, 63, 107, 108, 114, 128
Baker Cave, **85**, 86, 101, 139-141, **143**, 147
Bee County, sites in, 136, 142
Bell County, sites in, 147
Berclair Terrace, 142
Berger Bluff site, 132
Berlandier, Jean Louis, 50
Bexar County, sites in, 102, 106, 131, **134**, 138
biotic provinces, **35**
blade technologies, 158
Bonfire Shelter, 66, **67**, 98, 102, 132, 134, 138
bow and arrow, 96, 152
Brazos River, 47, 130
Brownsville, 63
Brownsville Complex, 73, 74, 107, 108, 122, 160
Buckhorn Ranch, 69, **71**
Buckner Ranch locality, 136, 142, 146
burial sites, 7, 69, **71**, **72**
burned rock middens, 63, **65**, 147

Cabeza de Vaca, Alvar Nuñez, 40, 50, 160
caches, 68-69
Calico Hills (California), 27

Cameron County, sites in, **72**, 73, **74, 75**, 106, 120
Campbell, T.N., 39, 46, 50
cannibalism, 42, 50, 54, 77
cataloging, artifact, 24, **180**
cave sites(see Baker, Cueva de la Candelaria, Scorpion)
cemetery sites, 7, **72**, 73, **74, 75, 76**, 77, **78, 79, 80**, 81, **82**, 154
Chaparrosa Ranch, 60, 65, 88, 90, 112, 149, 154, **155**
chert, 64, 88, 105, 130, 149, **155**, 157
Choke Canyon Reservoir, 61, 66, 112, 124, 150, 153, 166
chronology, 32, 156
clay dunes, 63, 130
Clovis Complex
  points, 28, 98, **99, 133, 135**
  sites, 28, 66, 131, 136
Coahuila (Mexico), 56, 110, **113, 161**
Coleto Creek, 132
color charts, 23
Colorado River, 47
Comal County, sites in, **97**, 131
Coon, Carleton S., 149
Corbin, James E., 63, 153
Corpus Christi, 50, 51, 54, 63, 77, 106, 108, 122, 160
Cuero Reservoir, **89**, 154
Cueva de la Candelaria, 110, 122

dart points
  defined, 94
  types of, 98, **99, 100**, 101, 102, **103**, 104
dating techniques, 25-26
dendrochronology, 25
Devil's Mouth site, 139, 147
Devil's River, 82, 139
DeWitt County, sites in, **89**
Dimmit County, sites in, 36, 39, 55, 58, 69, **71**, 98, 102, 105, 112, 124, **129**, 142
Duval County, sites in, 114, 131

Epstein, Jeremiah F., 136, 142, **144**
equus beds, 131
Espinosa, Fray, 47-48
Espiritu Santo Mission, 125
excavation techniques, 11-23
  base line, 15
  column sampling, **21**, 23
  datum point, 15

equipment, 14-15
grid system, 16, **20**
horizontal provenience, 15
instrument surveys, **20**
profiling, **21**, 23
  record forms, 18, **176, 177, 178, 179**
  screening, 18, **20**, 22
  soil sampling, 19, **21**, 22
  stratigraphy, 23
  vertical location, 17

field methods, 11-23
flake types, 90, **91**
flint (see chert)
Floyd Morris site, **72**, 73, **74, 75**, 120
Folsom Complex
  points, 28, **100**, 101, **133, 135, 145**
  sites, 28, 66, 132, 134
Formative period, 30-31
Frio County, sites in, 39, 98, 124, 142, **145**
Frio River, 39, 47, 66, 110, 159

Gateway Project, 164
Gatschet, A. S., 52, 128
Goddard, Ives, 39, 52
Goliad County, sites in, 102, **127**, 132, 143
Goliad ware, 125, **126, 127**
Golondrina Complex
  hearth (Baker Cave), 140, 141
  points, **100**, 101, **143, 145**
  sites, 86, 139, 142
Gonzales County, sites in, **89**
Graham, John A., 14
Granberg II site, 147, 149
Grullo Bay, 63, 114-115
Guadalupe River, 52, 53, 102, 114

Haynes, C. Vance, 27
Hays County, sites in, 51
hearths, 153-154, **155**
Hidalgo County, sites in, 52, 73, **74**
Hill, T. C., Jr., 65, 69, 124, 154
Historic period, 160, **161, 162, 163**, 164
Hondo Creek, 47
House, J. W., 69, 154

Indians, 38-56
  Apache, 38, 161
  Coahuilteco, 38-48, **41**, 50-53, 74, 124, 126
  Comanche, 38, 53-56, 108, 161
  intrusive groups, 56

Juanca, 39
Karankawa, 48, **49**, 50-51, 77, 125,
    127-128
languages, 39
Lipan Apache, 53-54, 56, 108
mission period, 160, 161
other hunting and gathering, 52-53
Pacuache, 39
Payaya, 39, 43, 45, 46-49
Tonkawa, 51-52, 108

Jetta Court site, 147
Jim Wells County, sites in, 36, 106, 124
Johnson, Charles II, 82, **83**, **117**
Johnson-Heller site, 142

Karnes County, sites in, 126, **126**, 166
Kendall County, sites in, 194
Kenedy County, sites in, 63, 130, **137**
kill-sites, 7, 66, **68**, 132
Kincaid Rockshelter, 128, 134
Kirchmeyer site, 63, 160
Kleberg County, sites in, 63, **76**

La Calzada Rockshelter, 136
La Jita site, 105
La Paloma locality, 136, **137**
La Perdida site, 154
La Salle County, sites in, 36, 58, 98, 110
Late Paleo-Indian period, 138-139, 146
Late Prehistoric period, 31, 51, 154,
    157-160
laws, antiquities, 81, 166
Levi Rockshelter, 132
Live Oak County, sites in, 34, **59**, 61, **62**,
    82, **83**, **116-117**, 124, 142, 154, 166
Loma Sandia site, 82, **83**, **116-117**
Los Olmos Creek, 114

McMullen County, sites in, 34, 37, 66, 94,
    107, 110, 124, 128, 142, 154, 159
Mariposa site, 60
Matagorda Bay, 50, 128
Maverick County, sites in, 55
Mazanet, 47
Medina River, 47, 86
mesquite, 34-35
mission Indian artifacts, **162**, 164
Montell Rockshelter, 132

Narváez expedition, 50
Newcomb, W. W., 38-39, 50, 84

Nueces County, sites in, 63, **78-79**, **80**, **81**
Nueces River, 50, 53, 86-87, **88**, 110
Nuevo Leon (Mexico), 84, 136, 142, **144**

occupation sites, 7-8, 57, **59**, 60, **61**, **62**
Odem site, 77
Oso Bay, 77
Oso Creek, 63, 77, 80, 128
Oso site, **78**, **79**
Oulline site, 58-59, 154

Padre Island, 106, 128
Paleo-Indian period
    North America, 28-29
    Texas, 66, 134, **148**
Pecos River, 82, 86, 101, 102
petroglyphs, 7, 82, 84
phytoliths, 22, 36, 150
pictographs, 7, 82, **84**
Plains-related tradition, 134
Plainview Complex
    points, 102, **103**
    sites, 66, 138
plant remains, 140
Pleistocene (Ice Age), 28-29, 35-36, 131
pollen, 19
Pre-Archaic period, 146-147, **148**, 149

radiocarbon techniques, 18, 26
Real County, sites in, 54, **65**
relic-collecting, 2, 165, 167
report preparation, 23-25, 173-175
Rio Grande Delta, 73, 108, 122, 160
Rio Grande gravels, 64, 88
Rio Grande Plain, 31
Rio Grande (River), 39, 47, 54-55, 82, 86,
    88, 98, 102, 107, 164
Rio Grande Valley, 107, 160
Robinson, Ralph, 36, 150
rock art sites, 7, 82, **84**
Rockport Complex, 160
rockshelter sites, **85**, 86 (see also Bonfire,
    Kincaid, La Calzada, Levi, Montell,
    Timmeron)

St. Mary's Hall site, 102, 134, 138
San Antonio, 47, 53, 102, 147
San Antonio de Valero, 164
San Antonio missions, **163**, 164
San Antonio River, 52, 114
San Bernardo Mission, **161**, 163, 164
San Francisco de Solano Mission, 52

San Isidro site, 142, **144**
San Juan Bautista Mission, 39, **163**, 164
San Lorenzo de la Santa Cruz Mission, 54
San Marcos Complex, 132
San Miguel Creek, 47, 142, **145**
San Patricio County, sites in, 80, 154
Scarborough site, 126
Scorpion Cave, 86, 159, 160
Sellards, E. H., 142, 146
shell middens, 62
shell-working technology, 160
sites
  definition of, 7
  designations, 10, 12-13
  excavation, 11-23
  kinds of, 7, 57-86
  locations in south Texas, 5
  survey techniques, 8-11, 167
Skillet Mountain #4 site, 66, **68**
Small Projectile Point Tradition, 136
snails, 18-19, 153
soil testing, 19-20
Southern Texas Archaeological Association, 1, 24, 48, 51, 168
South Texas Plains, 31
Spanish missions, 160, **161**, **163**, **164**
spearthrower, **94**, **97**, 152
Starr County, sites in, 57
Stewart site, 154
Stillhouse Hollow, 147
stone tool-making, 87-88, **89**, 90, **91**, 92, **93**

Tamaulipan biotic province, 31, 33, **35**
Tamaulipas (Mexico), 52
Terán expedition, 47
Texas A&I University, 136
Texas A&M University, 19-20, 94, 150

Texas Archeological Research Laboratory, 8
Texas Archeological Society 24
Texas Department of Highways and Public Transportation, 82, **83**, 134
Texas Historical Commission, 8, 89, 166
Texas Memorial Museum, **67**, **96**
Three Rivers, 82, 98, 101, 105, 115, 150, 166
Timmeron Rockshelter, 51
Toltec Culture, **129**, 130
Tortuga Flat site, 106
Travis County, sites in, 132, 147

Unland site, 106
University of Texas at Austin, 77, 136, **144**
University of Texas at San Antonio, 22, 60, 132
Uvalde County, sites in, 86, 105, **121**, 128, 132, 134, 147
Uvalde gravels, 64, 88, 90

Valsequillo Reservoir (Mexico), 27
Val Verde County, sites in, 66, **67**, **85**, 86, 87, 98, 101, 102, 132, 139, **143**
Varona, Salinas, 47
vertisols, 25
Victoria County, sites in, 120, 142, **145**, 149

Webb County, sites in, 39, 55, 58, 84, **84**, 86, 115
Willacy County, sites in, 150
Willeke site, 142
workshop sites, 7, 64

Zavala County, sites in, 39, 55, 60, **61**, 66, 69, **70**, **88**, 98, 102, 106, 110, 112, 124, **135**, 154, 161, 164